THIRD EDITION

The Basic Manual of
Fly-Tying

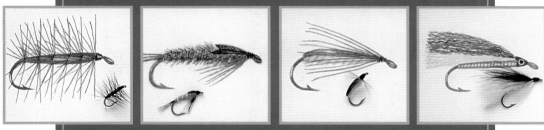

Fundamentals of Imitation

Paul N. Fling &
Donald L. Puterbaugh

Foreword by John Merwin
Foreword to Revised Edition by Nick Lyons

Sterling Publishing Co., Inc.
New York

TO ROD PATCH, DEAR FRIEND
AND A HELLUVA FLYFISHERMAN.

OTHER WORKS BY THE AUTHORS:
Expert Fly-Tying
Fly-Fisherman's Primer
Flyfishing Tips, Techniques, and Strategies of the Experts

Library of Congress Cataloging-in-Publication Data
Fling, Paul N.
   The basic manual of fly-tying : fundamentals of imitation / Paul N. Fling &
Donald L. Puterbaugh ; foreword by John Merwin. – 3rd ed.
        p. cm.
   Includes index.
   ISBN-13: 978-1-4027-3869-2
   ISBN-10: 1-4027-3869-2
   1. Fly tying. I. Puterbaugh, Donald L. II. Title.

SH451.F56 2007
688.7'9124–dc22

                                  2006029429

10 9 8 7 6 5 4 3 2 1

Published by Sterling Publishing Co., Inc.
387 Park Avenue South, New York, NY 10016
©2007 by Paul N. Fling and Donald L. Puterbaugh
Distributed in Canada by Sterling Publishing
c/o Canadian Manda Group, 165 Dufferin Street
Toronto, Ontario, Canada M6K 3H6
Distributed in the United Kingdom by GMC Distribution Services
Castle Place, 166 High Street, Lewes, East Sussex, England BN7 1XU
Distributed in Australia by Capricorn Link (Australia) Pty. Ltd.
P.O. Box 704, Windsor, NSW 2756, Australia

Printed in China
All rights reserved

Sterling ISBN-13: 978-1-4027-3869-2
        ISBN-10: 1-4027-3869-2

For information about custom editions, special sales, premium and
corporate purchases, please contact Sterling Special Sales
Department at 800-805-5849 or specialsales@sterlingpub.com

CONTENTS

THE BASICS

PATTERNS

FOREWORD TO THE THIRD EDITION

Fly-fishing and fly-tying can both be intimidating. Any novice who scratches the surface of either sport quickly finds so much available information that it's impossible to know where to start. For the would-be fly-tyer, the answer is simple: Begin with this book before you open any other.

For 30 years, Paul Fling and Don Puterbaugh's work has been a best-selling introduction to fly-tying. This newly revised third edition accounts for updates in tying materials, methods, and patterns, but doesn't dilute the reason for the book's long-term success. It is a basic book for beginners. That means really basic, a place to start from scratch with no prior knowledge, a place to find simple, straightforward answers and instruction.

In this digital age, it's unusual to find drawings instead of photographs used for instructional sequences. The simple reason is because drawings involve much more work to produce. In teaching fly-tying, though, drawings are actually more useful because the important details of each step can be made more evident. The placement of tying thread in each of Puterbaugh's exacting drawings is very precise and easily seen, for example. The net result is better instruction than could be obtained through pages of photos.

Both authors have an acute sense of what beginners need to know. Happily, that sense even extends to answers when things go wrong. It is common for new tyers to accidentally break the thread while tying, for example, or to have the wing of a partly constructed fly suddenly move out of kilter. One the book's early chapters deals specifically with those sorts of problems—a place to go when things don't seem to work according to plan. That's a rare approach among fly-tying books and a hugely useful one.

Back in the 1950s when I first started struggling with feathers and fur and fly-tying hooks, solid instruction was hard to find. My father was foremost in helping, having himself grown up with hands-on instruction from some local masters years before. I'll never forget his stopping at the kitchen table to pick up one of my new and coarsely minted streamer flies. He'd hold the hook and tug on the wing. Too often, the two would come apart. "Better work on that one some more," he'd say. I'd scowl and then try again. It was a long process.

Happily, your own evolution as a fly-tyer these days can be both shorter and more productive. Thanks to this updated classic you'll be doing things right at the very beginning and with enormous personal satisfaction.

—John Merwin
Fishing Editor, *Field & Stream* magazine

FOREWORD TO THE REVISED EDITION

More than fifteen years ago—in October 1976, to be exact—I received a proposal for a basic fly-tying book by Paul Fling and Donald Puterbaugh. I had by then spent nearly ten years developing the "Sportsmen's Classics" list at Crown Publishers, a group of books that then numbered slightly more than fifty. I looked carefully at the manuscript and would have been delighted to add it to that series.

But I had to write to the authors, of whom I knew nothing, "I'm afraid you're too late at Crown. I have a few last chores to perform and then will leave in early November; Crown has no plans to continue my series or to publish further books in the field."

And I had, at that time, no plans to work any longer in the publishing world; I had for many years taught English and American literature full-time at Hunter College and had edited full-time for Crown—along with doing some writing of my own, some professional writing, and far too little fishing. The authorities at Hunter had said I could no longer work at both jobs, and so I was leaving publishing. I thought—incorrectly—that I would never return.

I liked Paul Fling's manuscript and Don Puterbaugh's drawings very much; there was a genial, down-to-earth, no-nonsense quality about their work that I found engaging and very helpful. I told them that I thought the manuscript and line drawings were excellent, and I gave them a few suggestions about where to send them. (Having written a lot myself, and having gotten more anonymous printed rejection slips than I care to remember, I've always sent authors an actual letter, with a frank opinion. In most cases I never hear further from the authors.)

When the book appeared, published by Drake in 1977, I was very happy to see it in print, for it is one of the most helpful and truly practical basic fly-tying books ever produced. I was surprised when Paul told me recently that my letter had encouraged them to keep sending the proposal out, but I was not surprised when he told me that the book had sold 60,000 copies.

Now there is a new edition, which brings this important handbook nicely up to date. The new edition contains six new fly patterns, some new artwork and some that has been redone by Don, a thorough rewrite of the tools and materials sections (to accommodate the many advances in hackle, tools, the use of synthetic materials, and hooks), and a general honing and updating throughout.

The Basic Manual of Fly-Tying has always been a first-rate first book for beginning fly-tyers; now it will introduce a new generation to the happy and useful craft of tying flies, an art of great significance to all fly fishermen and a worthwhile and significant expansion of our lives astream.

Bravo, Paul and Don. I only wish I'd been fortunate enough to publish this fine book.

—Nick Lyons
New York City, 1992

PREFACE TO THE THIRD EDITION

When we assembled the revised edition of this book in 1992, we assumed that it would be our last visit. Here it is, fourteen years and a 100,000 copies or so later and we're back to it again, bald and/or gray, with arthritic fingers that still manage to "wind a fly."

The materials that are available, particularly in the realm of synthetics, have added so much to the arsenal of the fly-tyer. We've always advocated that there is no one material that must be used for a fly pattern. Logical substitution of materials should be such a part of a tyer's skills that it just happens as a normal occurrence. This has never been as important as it is now because of the ever-increasing number of materials available to the tyer. The use of natural materials has decreased over the past couple of decades simply because there are any number of synthetic materials that may be used in their place. That's true with one huge exception: HACKLE!

We made mention in the previous edition that commercially raised hackle had made great strides in satisfying our never-ending search for high quality capes and saddles. What is available to the fly-tyer today is beyond our dreams of even fourteen years ago: Capes that will tie dozens of #24 and smaller flies, and saddles that will have hackles to tie #22s—six or seven from each feather, that is! All of this, and in colors that are incredible. Makes a couple of old "feather benders" kick back in our rocking chairs in awe.

We can only wish for each of you a hint of the lifetime of pleasure we've enjoyed at the tying bench.

—Paul Fling and Don Puterbaugh

Paul and Don on their beloved Arkansas River in Colorado

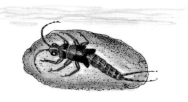

THE BASICS

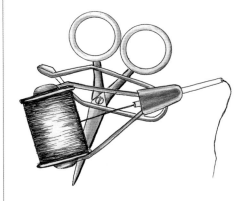

THE WORK AREA AND THE TOOLS

The Work Area

THE TYING SURFACE

The tying surface may be anything from the kitchen table to a highly refined, efficient bench built expressly for the purpose of tying flies. Whatever the size or location of the work area, however, there are a few points to consider that will make your fly-tying easier and more pleasant.

The desk, table, or whatever is used must provide a rigid support for the vise. Some steps in the tying process (spinning deer hair, for example) place a good deal of force on the hook, and this is transmitted to the table through the vise. Tying a difficult pattern is challenging enough without the handicap of a moving hook. In Illu. 1-1 you can see a workbench with a vise and magnifying lamp attached.

Also available are portable tying benches that are made to sit on a table or desktop. They have a support for the vise to be mounted on; spool-holders for threads, flosses, and tinsels; bottle holders for head cement and lacquers; and some even include storage room for a few necks. These are really handy if you don't have room for a permanent tying area.

STORAGE AND CONVENIENCE

You should have your fly-tying materials readily available. Parts storage boxes with compartments are sufficient when you haven't yet accumulated a large quantity of materials. You may have noticed some plastic sewing boxes at your local discount store. These are very good as they have built-in thread-holders on one tray, large compartments on another, and a deep storage area in the bottom.

The large tackle boxes that open on the side to reveal five or six drawers are especially nice. Each drawer is divided differently to hold varying types of materials, and the bottom drawer is sufficiently deep to hold a vise, necks, and other bulky items.

The important thing is to have your tools—at least the materials needed for immediate use, conveniently at hand. Nothing is quite as disconcerting as having to stop in the middle of tying a fly and go rummaging through shoe-boxes to find the material that you need to finish the fly.

1-1. Tying bench with vise and Daylight magnifying lamp.

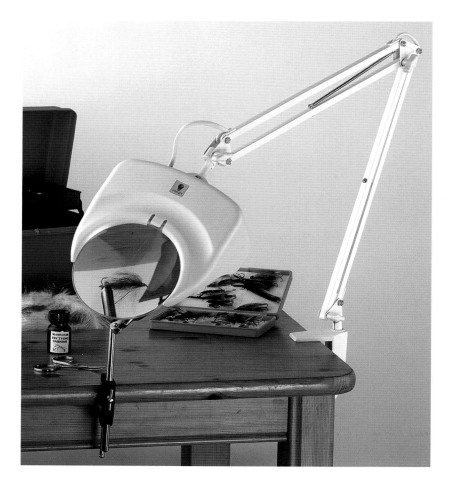

LIGHTING

The fly-tying area *must* be well lit, to prevent eyestrain and to ensure that subtle shades of color can be readily detected. Many tyers use a high-intensity light directed on the vise, but unless the surrounding area is also well lit, you will find that your eyes tire quickly because they must adjust each time you look away from the vise to the bench and back again.

There are really great lights made specifically for the tying bench. Some sit on their own bases next to the vise, others attach directly onto the base of the vise, and still others clamp onto the table. All are flexible, allowing the tyer to position the light to the best advantage. There are models that include magnifying lenses. The best of these accept bulbs that simulate the daylight spectrum so colors appear just as they will when your fly is in use.

The area behind the fly is important and is often overlooked as a cause of eyestrain. A very dark background makes colors appear brighter than they really are and may cause misinterpretation of shades of color. A white or very light background reflects a lot of glare into your eyes. Since you are looking somewhat down at the vise, the area under and just behind the vise is the background and you may need to experiment a bit to find a background that doesn't cause glare and illuminates the fly so it stands out.

The Basic Tools

The basic tools required by the fly-tyer are simple, relatively inexpensive, and really few in number. A few extra dollars spent to buy the best quality available will not only assure their long life, but also will help make your tying the joy it should be. The best tyer around can't do a good job and certainly can't enjoy tying on a shaky vise, or using hackle pliers that slip, or a bobbin that frays the tying thread. For the most part, the price of the tools available is directly proportional to their quality.

VISE

The vise is the tool used to hold the hook during the tying process. It may have a clamp base to attach to the edge of the tying table or a heavy pedestal base that sits on the work surface. The pedestal base is great if you must tie on a thick-edged table and is a real boon when you're on a fishing trip and tying in the camper or motel room, where a table with a top of the right thickness for a clamp may not be available. For the serious tyer with a permanent tying area, the clamp-type base provides a more rigid mounting.

There are many styles of vises available. Rear-lever vises (Illu. 1-2 and 1-3) are the most common type you are likely to see, and the most inexpensive

1-2. HMH rear lever vise.

1-3. Thompson rear-lever vise.

vises are of this type. Some top-of-the-line vises are rear-lever vises, however. Rear-lever vises have a cone-shaped throat and the jaws are drawn into the cone by a rear lever to close the jaws. A threaded collet is used to adjust how far the jaws are drawn into the cone and, thus, allows adjustment to hold differing sizes of hooks. The Thompson and HMH vises shown are rear-lever vises. Cam-action vises have the jaws held closed in the resting position and a lever is used to open the jaws and insert the hook. When the lever is released, the jaws close tightly on the hook. This style of vise needs no adjustment for hooks of different sizes. The Regal vise pictured in Illu.1-4 is a cam-action vise. Cam-action vises are generally more expensive than some of the rear-lever vises, but are quite convenient to use.

The Griffin vise is an example of a side-lock vise. It uses a knurled machine screw just behind the jaws to tighten on the hook. There is another adjustment screw at the rear to set the jaws to hold hooks within a certain size range (Illu. 1-5).

Another side-lock vise is the Renzetti, which is designed to hold the hook in position so it can rotate on its center axis. The rotating hook wraps

1-4. Regal cam-action vise.

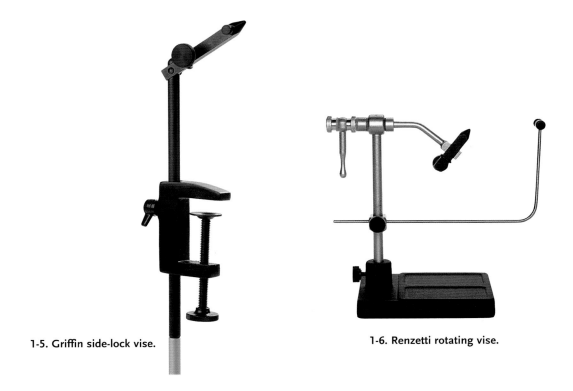

1-5. Griffin side-lock vise.

1-6. Renzetti rotating vise.

materials very quickly, as opposed to winding the materials on a stationary hook (Illu. 1-6).

Whichever base type and style of vise you choose, get the best your budget will allow.

BOBBIN

The bobbin holds the spool of tying thread. The thread passes from the spool out through a tube, allowing us to place the thread exactly where we wish, and since we don't handle the thread, the problem of fraying the thread with our rough hands is avoided. The greatest advantage of the bobbin, however, is its weight, which maintains tension on the thread while the tyer is between steps in the tying process.

A few tyers still tie, as we learned to do, without a bobbin. It is more difficult and slower to tie without a bobbin, and the resulting fly probably will not be very well constructed because of the difficulty of maintaining an even thread tension throughout the tying process.

The most common type of bobbin is the open type, which holds the thread spool between two legs of spring steel (Illu. 1-7). It allows for quick changing of the thread, quick retrieval of excess thread, and an easy means for adjusting tension by slipping a wrap of thread onto one of the legs. There are also models that mount the thread perpendicular to the tube and use a spring-loaded adjusting knob to apply the tension to the thread spool.

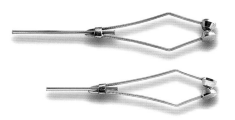

1-7. Open-leg bobbins.

A good bobbin will be nicely finished, the tube will be perpendicular to the spool, and the knobs that the spool rests between will be small enough to fit well inside the spool and yet large enough to hold the spring wires clear of the spool. The tube length is a matter of personal preference; Don prefers a long tube, and I prefer a short one. Several makers offer models that have ceramic tubes, while others offer them with titanium tubes—both of which are, of course, perfectly smooth and too hard for the thread to groove.

SCISSORS

There are still tyers who "tie in the hand" without a vise. It's quite possible to get by without a bobbin, and a bodkin isn't really indispensable, but I can't conceive of tying without scissors. Maybe some people have had their dentists do some special design work on their front teeth so they would work as scissors (that could have its use on the stream, too), but short of that, you have to have scissors to tie flies.

We tyers really need two pairs: a heavy pair for cutting lead, wire, rubber, and so on; and a smaller pair for the more delicate work of trimming hair, feathers, and the like. The quality of the heavy pair is not critical, and they need not be expensive. The fine pair should be the very best that you can afford (Illu. 1-8). You can get by with a pair of good-quality manicure scissors but they aren't cheap and generally the finger holes are quite small. Expect to pay a fair amount of money for a good pair of scissors, and don't buy any other kind. This is an item where quality is truly commensurate with price.

The basic scissors types for fly-tying are straight blade and curved blade (Illus. 1-9 and 1-10). Other variations are the scissors' length and the size of the finger holes. Straight blade or curved is a matter of choice, although each is better suited to some particular tasks. A pair of each is ideal, but one good pair of either is a better purchase than a cheap pair of each.

1-8. Short-bladed scissors.

For years I have used straight- and curved-blade iris scissors almost exclusively. They are available from medical supply houses and from most fly-tying suppliers. They are of very good quality with fine tips and comfortable finger holes. I have several pairs, but the pair on the tying bench is nearly thirty years old now and functions as flawlessly as the new ones. There are any number of really fine quality scissors made for the fly-tyer, including those with tungsten carbide cutting

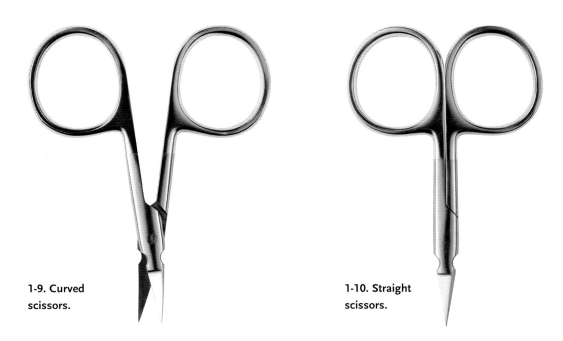

1-9. Curved scissors.

1-10. Straight scissors.

edges that will stay sharp for much longer than tempered steel blades. Once you've chosen good-quality scissors, take a moment and be certain that the finger loops are large enough to be comfortable.

HACKLE PLIERS

Hackle pliers are used to grasp the end of the hackle so that it can be wound on the hook. We also use them occasionally in the same manner for winding body material and to clamp on the tying thread to maintain tension after we have inadvertently cut the wrong thread and released the bobbin from this task.

We have found vises that work perfectly, bobbins that are flawless, and scissors of the same high standard, but the best of the hackle pliers that we have found still slip sometimes or occasionally cut the hackle. Undoubtedly, that's why there are so many types available.

The basic types of hackle pliers that you are likely to see are the English style, duplex style, teardrop, and hook types. The English pliers are made of spring wire and have overlapping tips of the same material in a flattened shape (Illu. 1-11). The duplex pliers are made of flat spring steel with attached pads. The pads may be of grooved metal; or one may be of metal and one of rubber; or both may be of rubber. The hook type of pliers

1-11. English style hackle pliers.

1-12. Hook style hackle pliers.

has a spring-loaded hook that grasps the hackle and pulls it against a sleeve or heavy wire (Illu. 1-12). Also available are rotating hackle pliers, which have duplex-style pliers on the end of a handle that can rotate as you wind the hackle.

For years we both used miniature English pliers and still have them handy on the tying bench. Don puts a piece of shrink tubing on one jaw of his pliers and strongly advocates using it. Shrink tubing, available from electrical supply houses, is rubberlike tubing that shrinks about 30% when heated. It works very well. I have one pair that I fixed this way, but the English pair that I like best is a pair that I took the time to smooth down to a perfect fit by rubbing a double sheet of emery paper through the closed jaws until they were perfectly mated. The hook types of hackle pliers are tenacious in gripping the hackle and cutting isn't much of a problem. They do use a larger amount of the hackle for holding, which makes them less than efficient when tying really small flies, however. The teardrop style has become the favorite with both of us, as they hold the hackle well without cutting it and are comfortable to use (Illu. 1-13).

BODKIN

The bodkin is simply a needle in a handle (Illu. 1-14). We use it to fluff up a dubbed body by picking, to help position a wing case, to split out the desired size of quill section for wings, and to do myriad other things. It is indispensable for placing a drop of head cement on our finished fly. You will see bodkins with plastic handles like a small screwdriver's, handles with a small eye on the end for hanging them on a hook at the edge or back of the bench, with metal handles of all shapes, with wooden handles, and with a large shepherd's hook on the end to be used for twisting dubbing—but the

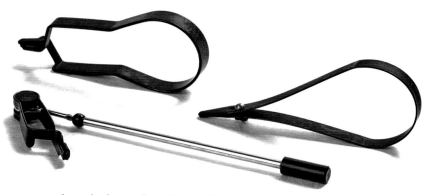

1-13. Teardrop, duplex, and rotating hackle pliers.

fact remains, a bodkin is just a needle in a handle. For many years I used one that was nothing more than a large sewing needle glued into a piece of ¹/₂" wooden dowel. I've moved up to a metal-handled one now, but its only real advantage is that the handle is hexagonal so it doesn't roll off the tying bench.

Other Tools

If you are gadget prone, you have a whole new world open to you as a tyer. In the next few paragraphs we will discuss some of the "auxiliary" tools that are available. All of them work, but none is a real necessity. If there is one particular step in the tying process that you are having trouble with, by all means try the tool designed for that step; it may be just what you are looking for. To assist you in evaluating the need for each, we will describe what the tool is used for and how it works.

HACKLE GUARD

The hackle guard is a small, funnel-shaped piece of metal with a hole in the center to slide over the eye of the hook and a slot through which to slip the thread (Illu. 1-15). It is used to hold the hackle back away from the eye of the hook to facilitate forming and tying-off the head of the fly more easily. Hackle guards work well, although they are time-consuming to use. Most tyers seem to abandon them after a short while.

MAGNIFYING GLASS

Attached to another vise stand, the magnifying glass is mounted on an arm that adjusts in all dimensions so that it can be positioned in front of the fly for focus and work clearance. It may be a godsend if you have poor eyesight or are tying very small flies. It does restrict the work area, however, and the change in size of everything when you look up from the glass is very distracting. I didn't have much use for a magnifying glass for the first forty years or so, but they've somehow become much more usable the last few years.

1-14. Bodkin.

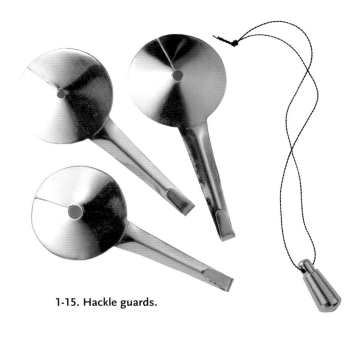

1-15. Hackle guards.

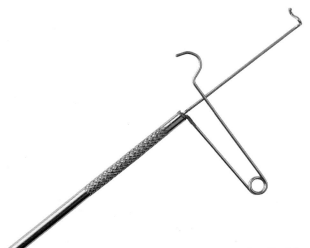

1-16. Whip finisher.

WHIP-FINISHER

Want to get a good knockdown argument going among a group of fly-tyers? Just bring up the subject of whip-finishers and state an opinion, pro or con. The tool is designed to assist in tying the knot we use to finish the head of the fly, a knot called the whip finish. The whip-finisher is a peculiarly shaped spring wire on a small handle. It is placed behind the eye of the hook, strung with the tying thread, and rolled between the fingers (Illu. 1-16). It works, and many very good tyers use them. The whip finish can be tied easily without the tool, although this knot has been an impasse for many a beginner. Neither Don nor I use one, primarily because it is slower than whip-finishing by hand. Also, when finishing by hand we can lay each wrap of thread exactly where we want it and better control the shape of the finished head. If you just can't get the knack of the whip finish from the descriptions and illustrations in this manual, you may want to give the tool a try.

HAIR STACKER

The hair stacker is a tube that can be opened on one end by removing a cap. To even the ends of a bunch of hair, insert the hair, replace the cap, and tap the hair stacker on the tying table. It is really a great help when tying patterns that use hair for the wing and/or tail. A hair stacker is very inexpensive and almost indispensable (Illu. 1-17).

DUBBING TOOL

There are some patterns that we wish to dress with a really thick, heavily dubbed body. There are also some furs that are very "hard" and slick and therefore difficult to form into dubbing. For both of these cases, a dubbing tool is the answer. To use the dubbing tool, we form a loop with our tying thread, place the material to be dubbed inside the loop, and then spin the loop closed by twisting the end. There are several different styles of tools for making the twisting of the loop easy: one type offered is a wire with a hook in the end to place in the loop. Another is Larry Walker's Dubbit and similar models (Illu. 1-18). The Dubbit offers the advantage of being large enough to hold onto easily and, since the center part is a bearing, we can just hold it by that part and spin the whole tool. The Dubbit is one of those great ideas that really works!

1-17. Wooden hair stackers.

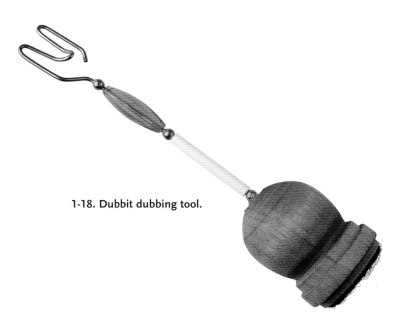

1-18. Dubbit dubbing tool.

1-19. Hackle gauge.

HACKLE GAUGE

A hackle gauge is a piece of metal or plastic that has been inscribed with lines to show the proper size of hackle to be used for a given size fly. The one that I have shows the hackle width for flies from sizes #4 to #24. Although the tool is a little awkward to use, it eliminates the common problem of over- or undersize hackle for a given fly size. It is much faster to attain the proper proportion directly from the tying hook—as will be shown in the tying instructions given in the patterns—but the tool does work for this purpose as well (Illu. 1-19).

BOBBIN THREADER

The bobbin threader is simply a long, thin loop of spring wire that is inserted through the bobbin tube (Illu. 1-20). The thread end is put in the loop and the wire is withdrawn, pulling the thread through the bobbin tube. It's not a required tool—as we'll explain later—but it is pretty handy to have on the tying bench.

TWEEZERS, PLIERS, AND MORE

There are many other tools that you may find useful to have on the bench, although they are not made specifically for fly-tying. Tweezers are helpful for picking up small hooks and are worth their weight in jungle cock for sorting #20 and #22 hooks that get spilled together. A small pair of needle-nosed pliers is useful for working with wire that is being used for body material and nearly indispensable when tying bead head nymphs. A razor blade or scalpel has many uses, and a rubber eraser is an aid in stripping peacock herl. This list is limited only by your ingenuity and bench space.

1-20. Bobbin threader.

THE
MATERIALS

Nearly every creature that walks or flies is a source of material to the fly-tyer. Our discussion will be limited to those that are readily available and most frequently called for in the standard patterns. The most important lesson that we hope you will learn from this section is the substitution of materials. There are those who will not tie a pattern with anything but the materials that originally were used, which are called for in the pattern description. Our desire is that you will become a fly-tyer, not just a pattern reproducer. Surely, most of the patterns presently used are effective, but that effectiveness need not be reduced because you have substituted a different kind of thread, or hook, or even type of wing. Fish feed on insects, *not on artificial flies*, and as long as the fly that you are producing is an accurate representation of that insect, it is going to work.

With this in mind, our approach will be to describe the materials available to you for use in the various parts of a fly, so that you may have some idea of which materials may be substituted in a recognized pattern and, more importantly, so that you will have basic knowledge of the characteristics of the materials and can develop your own patterns based on the insect life found in the streams that you fish.

Hooks

We are forever dismayed by the list of hooks recommended in most tying manuals. Hooks are the most expensive part of the finished fly, and to imply to beginners that they must have 20 or 30 different types of hooks and a range of all sizes of each is not only a discouragement, but is out-and-out foolish. At least 90% of all flies can be tied, with no loss of fish-taking ability, on 5 types of hooks. Again, the point is, is there a reason for using a particular hook, or does the pattern call for it just because that was what the originator happened to use? As long as the hook that you use is of the right length to accurately represent the insect and is of the right type (wet or dry), we can assure you that the fish doesn't care about the number on the box from which it came. As an example, the tackle shop where we used to work and run our classes sold more than 1000 dozen flies a year and carried a stock of more than 150 patterns; we used a total of 7 hook types.

In our discussion of hooks, and particularly hook designations, we are not referring to any particular brand. The sizing from brand to brand is very similar and the general designations (long, short, stout, fine) are common across all the makers.

WET HOOKS

The hook used for wet flies and nymphs is made of heavier wire than that used for dry flies, so that the additional weight will help to sink the fly. The Tiemco TMC3769 and TMC3761, Mustad 3906 and 3906B and Daiichi 1550 are commonly used for wet flies and nymphs. The Tiemco TMC3761, Mustad 3906B, and Daiichi 1710 are 2X long hooks and are used for imitations that require a little longer body length. See page 50 for a demonstration of hook proportions.

DRY HOOKS

To aid in allowing the dry fly to float, the hook used for tying dry flies is made of finer wire and is, therefore, lighter. So that as much strength as possible can be retained in the hook, the bend area is forged flat. The Tiemco TMC 100, Mustad 94840, and Daiichi 1100 are standard dry-fly hooks while the Tiemco TMC 5212 and TMC 200R, the Mustad 9671 and 9672, and the Daiichi 1280 are used for patterns that require a longer shank. These longer hooks will also double as short streamer hooks and may be used for tying imitations of long-bodied nymphs, such as stoneflies.

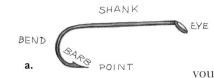

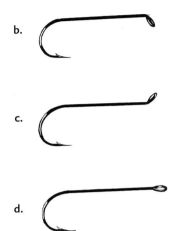

2-1. Hooks.
(a) hook parts.
(b through d)
hook eye shapes:
(b) turned-down eye;
(c) turned-up eye;
(d) ring eye.

There are many other types and makes of hooks that you may use just as well as these. And again, that is the point: you are not restricted to any particular make or type. Just be sure that the hook you are using will give you a finished fly of the right size and proportion to complement the way the fly is to be fished.

HOOK SIZES, SHAPES, AND DIMENSIONS

Hook sizes are designated by numbers; the size of the hook decreases as the hook number grows larger; e.g., a #20 hook is smaller than a #14. The size of the hook *only* refers to the width of the gap (or gape) of the hook; that is, the distance between the point of the hook and the shank. Hooks used for freshwater flies are normally tied in the size range from #4 to #28, although they are available in both larger and smaller sizes; usually, fly-tying hooks are only available in even-numbered sizes. Remember, hook size is only an indicator of the gap width of the hook.

Hook length is designated by X's; a #14-2X long hook is a #14 with a shank length of a hook two sizes larger (a #12). A #14-2X short is a #14 with a shank length of a hook two sizes smaller (a #16).

Wire size is designated in basically the same way; a #14-2X fine is a #14 made from wire normally used for a hook two sizes smaller (a #16). A #14-2X stout is made from the same wire as a standard #12. As you can see, there are really a great number of variations available for a hook of a given size.

Another variable among hooks is the shape of the eye (Illu. 2-1). The most common is the turned-down eye (TDE), in which the eye is bent down from the shank of the hook toward the point. The turned-up eye (TUE) is another commonly used hook and is of some advantage for very small hooks as the eye is turned away from the point and gives more clearance for hooking the fish. The ring eye—with the eye in line with the shank—is most commonly seen on streamer hooks, although it is beginning to be used more and more for dry flies, particularly in the very small sizes, where it offers improved gap clearance (like the TUE) and a better hook setting characteristic, since the strike is in line with the shank of the hook.

The shape of the bend is the least important variable among hooks. The most common bend shapes are the perfect bend, the sproat bend, and the limerick bend. The perfect bend has the bend formed as part of a circle, the sproat bend is slightly parabolic, and the limerick has a very pronounced parabolic shape to the bend.

As you can see, the variety of hooks available to the fly-tyer is staggering. The only thing of importance, though, is the finished fly, so don't become too concerned about using a particular hook as long as the finished fly is of the proper proportion for the size of the insect you are imitating and as long as the weight complements how the fly will be fished.

Thread

THREAD COLORS

The tying manuals really get carried away here. One pattern book that I have lists approximately 60 patterns, and you would need 18 different spools of thread to follow the instructions for tying those 60 patterns. Hogwash! On a properly tied fly, the only thread that is visible to the fish is the head, and we have no evidence that the color of the head has any effect on the fish-attracting ability of the fly. If it is more aesthetically pleasing to you for the thread to be of the same color as the major portion of the fly, by all means use it, but don't feel that you have to do without a particular pattern because you don't happen to have any primrose-colored thread on hand.

THREAD SIZES

Thread sizes are indicated by letters of the alphabet. Sizes A through E are used for rod wrapping, but are of little use to the fly-tyer. Sizes smaller than A are designated by "oughts" (zeros); two-ought (00) is one size smaller than A, and three-ought (000) is the next smaller, and so on, down to twelve-ought (000000000000). Instead of listing six ought as 000000, the common method is to use the designation 6/0. For most tying, thread of 6/0 or 8/0 is used, although thread is available as fine as 12/0 and as heavy as A. A would only be used for large flies such as bass bugs, larger streamers, and saltwater patterns.

OUR CHOICES

We use 6/0 and 8/0 Uni-Thread for all of our tying, although 3/0 Monocord isn't a bad choice for the beginner as it is a little more break-resistant than the smaller threads. As to color, we use two colors for at least 90 percent of the flies we tie: black and green. We use green when we tie a weighted nymph or wet fly so that we can readily identify it in our fly boxes, since we tie many of these patterns in both weighted and unweighted versions.

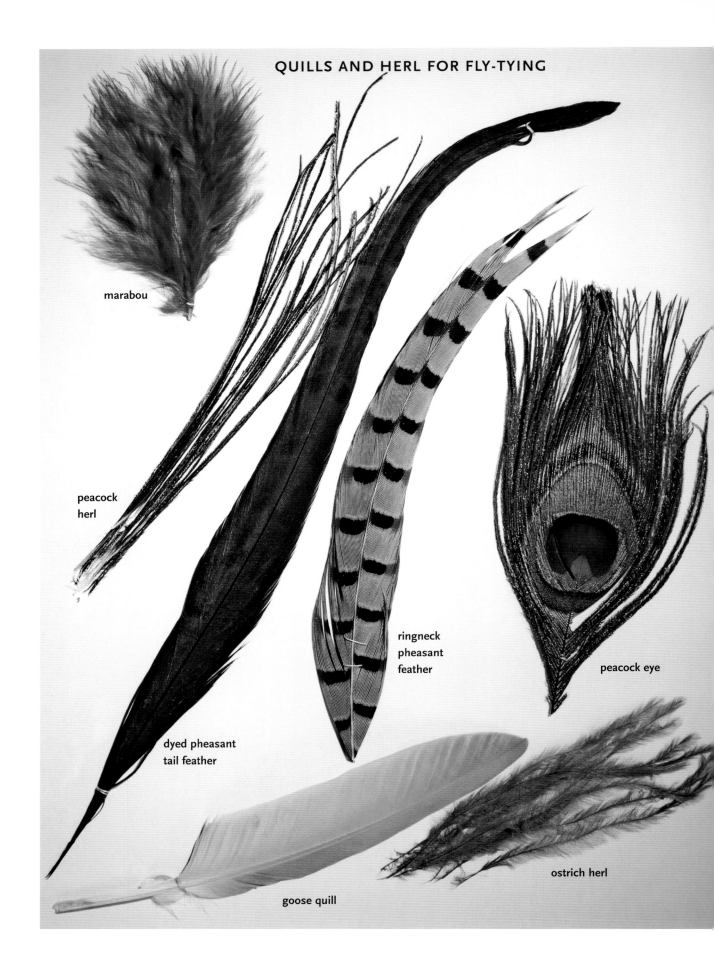

marabou

peacock
herl

dyed pheasant
tail feather

ringneck
pheasant
feather

peacock eye

goose quill

ostrich herl

Tailing Materials

HACKLE FIBERS

The traditional material for use as tails on flies is hackle fibers, although in the western United States you are just as likely to find hair being used. The best hackle fibers for tails are from large neck hackles or saddle hackles. For dry flies, a very stiff hackle is needed, so the fibers are taken from near the upper end of the hackle feather. For a wet fly or nymph, a softer hackle is desirable, and it is selected from a soft hackle or from further down the stem of a dry-fly hackle, where it is softer and has more web.

HAIR

There is no end to the types of hair that may be used for the tailing of a fly. Here in the western United States we use more hair for tails than hackle because of the generally bigger, faster water we have to fish and the additional support that is needed. The heavier, rougher water also means that we needn't be quite so delicate in our imitations. Elk and javelina hair are exceptionally good tailing materials, as are the coarse guard hairs of many of the water dwellers, such as muskrat. In the selection of hair for tails, keep in mind what you want as a finished product. If you are tying a dry fly, you want the stiffest hair you can find, and if you are tying wet flies or nymphs, you want something softer so that you get a "swimming" action from the tail.

SYNTHETICS

There are also some synthetic materials that lend themselves for use as tailing material. "Micro-fibetts" (nylon fibers similar to the bristles of a paint brush) are ideal for tying really small dry flies and thin silicone rubber strips are used on some attractor style patterns.

OTHER TAILING CHOICES

For a well-defined tail on nymphal patterns, we often tie in two sections of turkey quill, which are then separated with wraps of tying thread and lacquered. Sections of any quill material may be used in a like manner. For a separated tail on dry flies such as the Swisher-Richards "no-hackle" patterns, face whiskers from a rabbit or groundhog are ideal, as they are very stiff and are long enough to be easily used. The material itself is of no great importance so long as the desired imitation is achieved. Calf tail (also called *kip* and *impala*), squirrel tail, and bucktail are also used on some patterns.

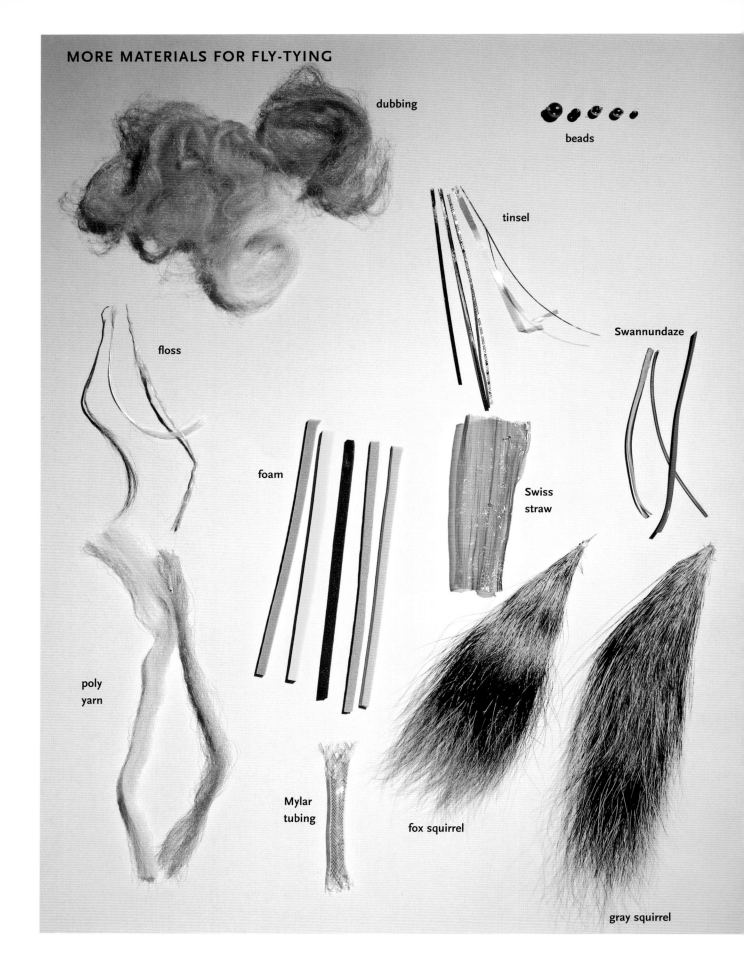

dubbing

beads

tinsel

floss

Swannundaze

foam

Swiss straw

poly yarn

Mylar tubing

fox squirrel

gray squirrel

Body Materials

Practically every material used by the tyer can be employed for the formation of the body of the fly.

QUILLS AND HERL

You can use the center quill of a hackle by stripping off all the fibers and wrapping the quill around the hook. This gives a nice, segmented shape to the finished body.

You can strip peacock herl and use it in the same manner, and if you choose the herl from the eyed portion of the peacock feather, it will give you a segmented effect, because of the longitudinal coloring of the quill. This, by the way, is the technique normally meant when a pattern calls for a "quill" body.

HAIR

We use the hollow hair from members of the deer family (elk, deer, antelope, moose, etc.) for making "hair" bodies. Bunches of deer hair are tied in, and as the thread is tightened, the hair is allowed to spin around the hook and flares away from the hook shank. We tie in succeeding bunches in the same manner, until the desired body length is obtained, which we then trim into shape. This body type yields a dry fly with outstanding floating qualities, because the hair we have used is hollow.

MANMADE MATERIALS

There are many manmade materials that we use for the bodies of flies. Polypropylene, whose fibers have a specific gravity that is less than water's, and therefore float, is available in many forms, including yarn, loose dubbing material, and pressed sheets from which fibers are teased, to be used as dubbing material. Latex sheet material is used extensively for the bodies of nymphs, larvae, and pupae. Thin foam (smooth and fuzzy) is used for body materials, as is a delightful soft, stretchy, clear "plastic" cord called Larva Lace, which is available in a whole series of important colors.

Textiles furnish a wide selection of body materials, including floss, thread, tinsel, Mylar, yarns, and chenilles. The most used body material, however, is dubbing.

DUBBING

The term "dubbing" describes both the process of spinning a fur onto the tying thread to form a fur "yarn" and the yarn thus formed. We wind the dubbed thread onto the hook to form the body of our fly. A dry fly tied with a dubbed body floats extremely well when the dubbing is treated with dry-fly floatant, and a wet fly or nymph sinks equally well when the dubbing soaks up water. A dubbed body's greatest asset, however, is that it produces a lifelike, translucent body due to the fine fibers extending from the edges of the body. The furs for dubbing come from the soft underfur of many animals, including rabbit, muskrat, mink, and fox. The synthetic dubbing materials are used in the same manner, and the soft down from waterfowl may be handled the same way.

If you are tying a standard pattern, the directions will tell you what type of body material to use, and if you are trying to duplicate an insect that you have found, keep in mind that the type of body material you use should be chosen to best represent the natural insect. If you want to imitate a hard-bodied nymph, you might choose latex, Larva Lace, tinsel, or wire. If, on the other hand, you are tying to represent a fuzzy caddisfly larva, you might select wool yarn, chenille, or dubbing.

Experiment with all the materials that you can get, so that logical substitution will become second nature.

Winging Materials

Basically, there are four types of wing construction: quill wing, rolled wing, hair-wing, and hackle-tip wing.

QUILL WING

2-2. Example of an upright quill wing, used for a dry fly (Pattern 8).

A quill wing is made from sections of a quill feather tied in on each side of the hook. They may be tied in either an upright or a "down" position (aligned horizontally). The upright position is used when tying dry flies. The upright position is used in Pattern 8, for example (shown here as Illu. 2-2). The down position is used when tying wet flies; see Pattern 7, for example. Duck quill feathers are the ones most commonly used, although goose feathers and the flight feathers from many smaller birds will also provide the quill segments for wings. The quill wing provides a good mayfly silhouette, but is not very durable.

ROLLED WING

2-3. A rolled wing (Pattern 10).

A rolled wing is made from a bunch of soft body feathers tied in on the top of the hook as a clump and then divided with the tying thread, or sometimes trimmed to shape (used in Pattern 10, for example, and shown here as Illu. 2-3). The rolled wing is considerably more durable than the quill wing.

Mallard side feathers are the most commonly used material, but soft hackle fibers work well, as do the body feathers of many of the pheasants. Many standard patterns call for a rolled wing constructed from "lemon wood duck." This is the flank feather from a wood duck and is the premium feather for this type of wing construction, but unfortunately it is in extremely short supply and therefore quite expensive. Mallard flank feathers dyed to this color are the common substitution material. If you or any of your friends are duck hunters, you should have no trouble getting mallard feathers and perhaps even a "woodie."

We also tie some patterns whose wings are constructed very much like a rolled wing, but we use polypropylene yarn as the winging material. The wing on these "poly-wing" flies is extremely tough and long-lasting. The poly wing is used in Pattern 28, shown here as Illu. 2-4.

2-4. A polypropylene (poly) wing (Pattern 28).

HAIR WING

The hair wing is the most durable of the wings made from natural materials and is commonly used on streamers and wet flies, as well as on dry-fly patterns. Calf tail, bucktail, squirrel tail, and mink tail are the most common sources of hair, although the body hair of deer, elk, bear, and many other animals also is used. Pattern 12 is an example of a pattern with a hair-wing, shown here as Illu. 2-5.

2-5. Example of a hair wing (Pattern 12).

HACKLE-TIP WING

As the name implies, hackle-tip wings are tied using hackle tips. This is a great place to use up some of those hackle feathers that are too large for most of the flies we tie. Two matched hackles are chosen, and a tip of each, of the right length for the fly we are tying, is cut from the hackle stem. These are tied in on either side of the hook to form the wings. The hackle-tip wing makes a very attractive fly with a fair durability rating. Pattern 9 is an example of a hackle-tip wing, shown here as Illu. 2-6.

2-6. Example of a hackle-tip wing (Pattern 9).

The quill wing, rolled wing, poly wing, and hackle-tip wing are most often used for representing mayflies; the hair wing is more commonly used to suggest the "over-the-back" wing of the caddisflies and stoneflies.

WING-CASE MATERIALS FOR NYMPHS

Although it does not have fully developed wings, the nymph does have a case on top of the thorax that contains the developing wings; it is called, appropriately enough, a wing case. Many different materials can be used for representing the wing case, but some of the most common are: narrow sections of

2-7. Example of nymph, showing wing case (Pattern 4).

turkey quill, sections of duck or goose quill, Swiss Straw (a synthetic material available in most fabric shops as well as fly shops), and a strip of latex. An example of a nymph with wing case can be seen in Pattern 4, shown here as Illu. 2-7.

STAYING FLEXIBLE IN YOUR CHOICES

It's important to understand that there are very few fly-tying materials for which there are not usable substitutes, either in natural materials or synthetics. This is especially true in the area of synthetic materials. Very few synthetic materials are created specifically for fly-tying. Almost always, the material was developed for some other purpose and tyers just found a way to use it. The problem is that each of the material suppliers will purchase the material in bulk and repackage it for the tying world. And every one of them will give it a different name! Don't get hung up on needing a product by a particular name. We'll be stressing this point of material substitution throughout the book, but please accept the fact that you are tying to represent an insect or baitfish and that there are many materials you can use to yield an effective end product.

Hackle Feathers

KINDS

Hackle feathers (also referred to as "hackle") may be purchased loose by the package, but more commonly are purchased as a "cape" (also called a "neck") or "saddle"; the hackles are still attached to the skin of the chicken. The latter gives the tyer a selection of all sizes of hackle and makes the sorting much easier, as Mother Nature has provided the ultimate packaging method. In addition to the ease of handling, buying hackles by the cape or saddle also offers substantial cost savings.

Hackle comes in several grades of quality, from "wet" (very soft) to "Number 1" or "platinum" (very stiff). The type of hackle that you need is dependent on the type of fly you are tying. A wet-fly hackle should be very soft to give a more enticing action to the finished fly, whereas a dry fly needs the stiffest hackle available, as the hackle is the prime support for keeping the fly afloat. Wet-fly hackle comes from hen chickens and dry-fly hackle comes from roosters.

Other than their appropriate uses, the biggest difference between a wet-fly cape and a good dry-fly cape or saddle is cost. A very good wet-fly cape will cost about 10% as much as a premium dry-fly cape or saddle. We all probably use too much hackle of dry-fly quality because there is a tendency to buy only dry-fly hackle. The reason for this may well be that all of the qualities we look for in a good dry cape or saddle are absent in a good wet cape, and it is just not very impressive. Occasionally, feathers from birds other than a chicken are used as hackle, but only for the soft hackle found on nymphs, streamers, and wet flies.

QUALITY, SOURCES, AND GRADES OF HACKLE

A high-quality dry-fly hackle will be very long in relation to its width, have a thin stem and, when flared, the fibers will be very stiff. At the time that the first edition of this manual was written (1977) the vast majority of necks that we tyers used were imported from Asia. Of the tremendous numbers that were imported, a very small proportion were of dry-fly quality, and even fewer had hackles with which you could tie the sizes smaller than #18. As the number of tyers increased, the market became large enough to make it economically feasible for roosters to be raised specifically for their hackles.

When the second edition was published in 1992, the commercial hackle firms were starting to produce really top quality dry-fly necks in sufficient quantity to meet the needs of the tying world. Additionally, they began producing saddle hackles of true dry-fly quality. We now have saddle hackles that can tie flies as small as #22—and we can tie six or eight flies out of each feather! The availability of saddles of this quality has made the greatest change in the fly-tying world in the last half-century. In fact, it has become difficult to even find a listed source for imported hackle in dry-fly grades. It just can't begin to compete with the quality of the commercially raised hackle.

The companies that commercially raise hackle grade it for quality and, in our experience, do a very accurate job. They grade the hackle from their best grade to #3; the major difference is in the number of hackles on the neck or saddle, particularly in the smaller sizes. Unless you are tying a lot of very small flies, the #2 and #3 necks or saddles will serve you quite well. Some companies also package their necks and saddles in halves and quarters and in packs containing enough individual hackle to tie one hundred flies. This allows the tyer to have a greater assortment of colors and markings without an enormous outlay of cash.

Since it is difficult to raise roosters without hens, we now also have high-quality wet-fly necks readily available from the commercial hackle farms.

Although the ideal wet-fly hackle would be relatively long for its width and have a thin stem, these particular attributes aren't as prevalent as with the dry-fly hackle. But, since we typically use fewer wraps of hackle on a wet fly, these features aren't of great importance. What is important though is for the hackle fibers to be very soft to impart that desired lifelike action to our flies.

COLORS OF HACKLE

Fly-tying has a long history, and nowhere are we more reminded of this than when we talk about the colors and markings of hackle. Let's talk about the colors first. To some degree the typical quality of a hackle seems to be tied to its color, but even these general "truths" have become less true with the advent of commercially raised hackle, in which the geneticist has bred quality into colors that are naturally soft. As we talk about the colors and their inherent quality, recognize that commercially raised hackle has, to a great extent, eliminated the classic relationship between color and quality. There are, however, degrees of fiber stiffness that are still inherent in the different colors of hackle, they just are not as pronounced as in the past. In short, we now have superb dry-fly hackle in all colors. Even the "soft" colors are as good as the very best hackles of the past.

Black: Black is found as a natural color, but generally the hackle tends to run on the soft side. The commercial raisers do come up with decent quality blacks, though, and also dye other, more inherently stiff feathers to black.

Coachman: A very dark brown shade of hackle is called *coachman*, which runs toward being on the soft side; again, there is good coachman available from the hackle companies.

Dark Ginger: Dark ginger is somewhat lighter than coachman and has a reddish cast. Dark ginger and ginger are probably the colors used most often and are available in very good quality.

Ginger: Ginger is the color of that spice, a medium brown with a definite reddish tint. It is naturally of good quality and the ginger currently available is near perfect. Ginger is sometimes listed as just "brown."

Light Ginger: Light ginger is about the color of a weak cup of tea. It is available in very good quality.

Cream: Cream hackle ranges from just darker than white to a honey color. Although cream is naturally soft, the hackle raisers have come up with strains of chickens that do produce really good hackle.

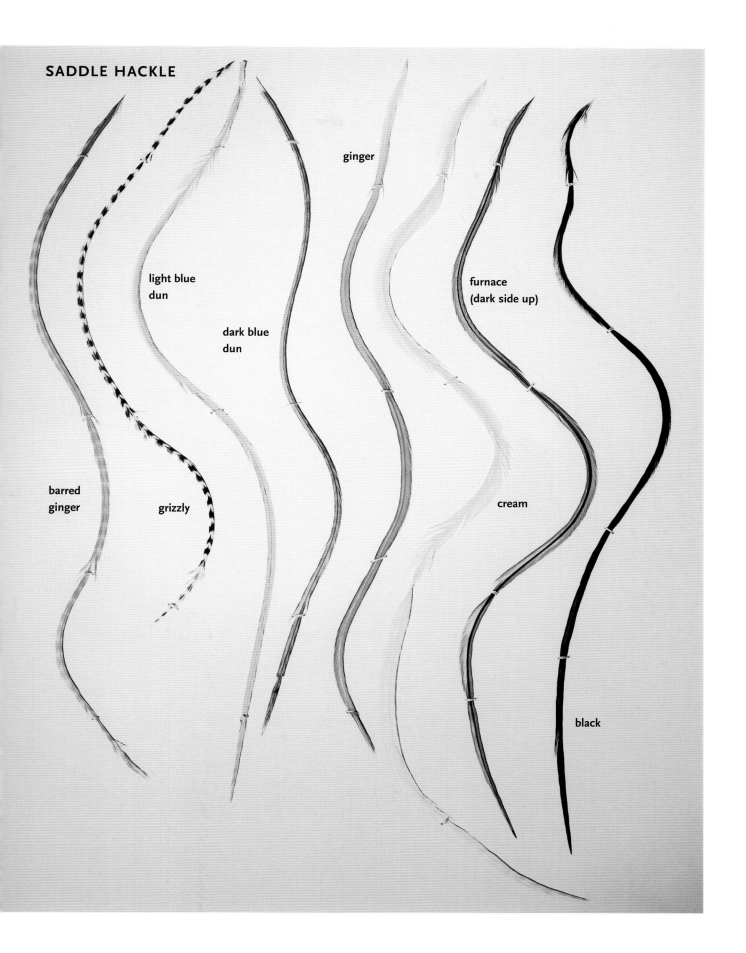

SADDLE HACKLE

ginger

light blue
dun

dark blue
dun

furnace
(dark side up)

barred
ginger

grizzly

cream

black

White: White is a very common color of hackle and, although notorious for being soft, it is readily available from the commercial growers. There's not much call for white in our insect imitations, though.

Dun: The premier color for fly-tying is called *dun*. It is a rather nondescript gray, which may have undertones of blue, bronze, brown, or olive. Because the coloring of dun hackles so closely matches the natural insect colors, they are often called for in patterns and are a good choice for many imitations. Until recently, a good-quality natural dun was so rare that most tyers had never seen one. Now duns are readily available, including all of the undertones.

MARKINGS OF HACKLE

Terms like badger, furnace, and coch-y-bonddu sound strange to our ears, but are so firmly embedded in the language of tyers that it is important for you to understand their meaning. These terms are used to describe the markings on the individual hackle feathers.

Furnace: A furnace hackle is a hackle in the color range of ginger to coachman with a black center stripe.

Coch-y-Bonddu: A furnace hackle with the addition of black edges (called a "list") is called a *coch-y-bonddu*.

Badger: A hackle in the color range from white to light ginger with a black center stripe is called a *badger*.

Variants: A variant, in its strictest definition, is any hackle with more than one color present. In the vernacular of the fly-tyer though, it generally means a barred hackle. Variants are found in the full color range from white to coachman, with the most common being ginger barred with black and white. Variants are probably underused by most of us. This may be because the term has no absolute definition and, therefore, is difficult to describe in a pattern. Variants provide a breakup of color that is really imitative of the coloring found on most aquatic insects. Generally, they are of very good quality.

Grizzly: A variant that is black or gray with white bars has a special name: *grizzly*. Grizzly (also called Plymouth Rock because it comes from a rooster of that breed) is one of the most-used hackles. The very best hackle that I have seen has been grizzly. All of the commercial growers raise grizzly and the quality is excellent.

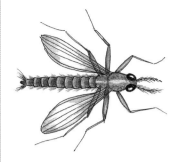

THE INSECTS THAT WE IMITATE AND THEIR LIFE CYCLES

Overview

To the fly fisherman, the four important groups of aquatic insects are the mayflies, caddisflies, stoneflies, and midges. Other insects that trout feed on may be of occasional importance, but these four account for the bulk of its diet. We will look at some of the others later.

Aquatic insects progress through several stages during their life cycle. The changes in form they undergo are called *metamorphoses* and, depending on the insect, the metamorphosis may be complete or incomplete. Complete metamorphosis consists of the progression from egg to larva, pupa, and adult. In incomplete metamorphosis, the insect passes through only three stages: egg, nymph, and adult. The larva looks entirely different from the adult. Mayflies and stoneflies undergo incomplete metamorphosis; caddisflies and midges progress through all four stages of development.

The stages in the life of an insect are what we are trying to imitate with flies; they are the reason that we tie wet flies, nymphs, and dry flies. Regardless of the type of metamorphosis, all stages but the adult stage of the abovementioned insects are spent in the water. Wet flies and nymph imitations are used to represent the subaquatic forms. Dry flies are meant to be representative of the adult stage. In the following pages, the life cycles of the mayfly, caddisfly, stonefly, and midge are covered in detail.

Life Cycle of the Caddisfly (Trichoptera)

Caddisflies go through complete metamorphosis: from egg, to larva, to pupa, and then to adult.

The underwater larval stage of most caddisfly species is spent inside a case constructed of either pieces of sand or of vegetable matter. The case of the larva is open on one end, and the insect can extend its head and thorax from the case. In some instances the larva can transport its case with it as it moves around to feed on microscopic vegetable matter in the stream. A few species are free-swimming and attach themselves to underwater rocks or debris with a thin filament to keep from being washed away.

■ 3-1. LIFE CYCLE OF THE CADDISFLY

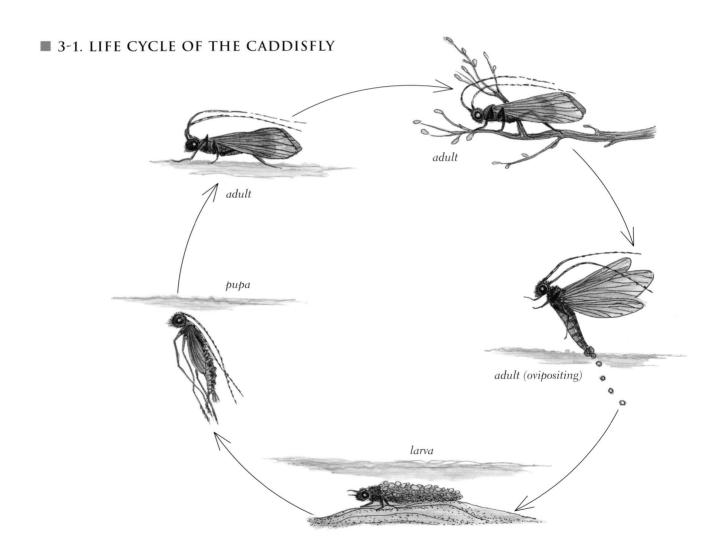

adult

adult

adult (ovipositing)

pupa

larva

When the caddisfly goes into pupation, it seals up its case except for a very small hole that allows just a trickle of water to flow through. During pupation, the wings, legs, and antennae develop and the insect attains the adult form. When pupation is complete, the caddisfly rises to the surface, breaks through the surface film, and immediately flies away from the stream.

The adult caddisfly mates while at rest away from the stream. The females then return to the stream and deposit their eggs, either by dropping the eggs to the surface, by alighting on the surface and releasing the eggs, or by crawling down into the stream and leaving the eggs attached to sticks, stones, or stream debris (Illu. 3-1).

Life Cycle of the Mayfly (Ephemeroptera)

Mayflies undergo incomplete metamorphosis, passing from egg, to nymph, to adult. They are unique, however, in that there are two forms in the adult stage. The dun (subimago) stage is seen just after emergence, while the spinner (imago) stage is seen during the mating flight; the final molt from dun to spinner occurs away from the stream, normally in the surrounding brush.

Mayfly nymphs are categorized by the type of water in which they are found, as each group has particular physical characteristics that are adapted to that type of aquatic environment. "Crawlers" are found in moderate stretches of the stream, "clingers" are found in fast stretches, "swimmers" are found throughout the range from fast to slow water, and "burrowers" are found most often in slow stretches of water.

As the nymphal stage draws to a close, the nymph's wing case darkens and swells as the wings mature inside. It is during this time that the nymph starts its migration to the water's surface to hatch. At the surface, the wing case splits open and the adult dun emerges. This is the stage that we imitate with upright-wing dry flies. Once the wings are set firm, the insect flies from the surface into the nearby brush, where sexual development continues and the final molt into the spinner stage occurs.

The spinners then return to the stream, where they can be seen in swarms above the water. The females seek out partners; the pairs leave the swarm and mate in flight. The females then deposit the eggs into the stream: some drop them from above the stream, some species lie prone on the surface

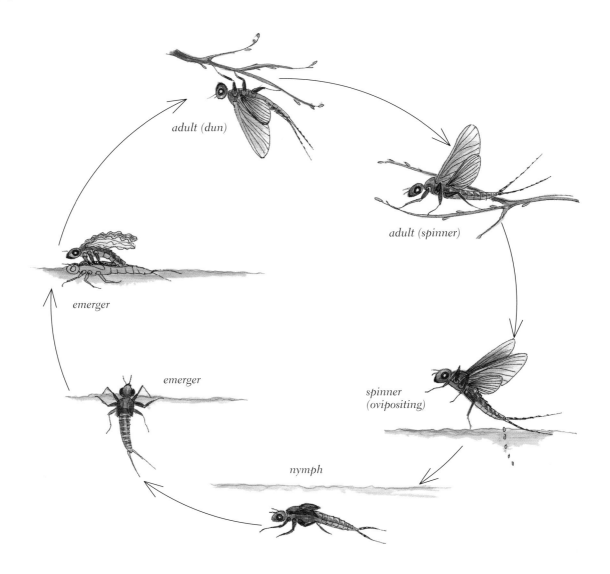

adult (dun)

adult (spinner)

emerger

emerger

spinner (ovipositing)

nymph

film and release their eggs, and some species crawl back into the water to leave their eggs. Both the females and the males then perish and fall onto the surface of the water with their wings in the spent (outspread) position (Illu. 3-2).

Life Cycle of the Stonefly (Plecoptera)

Stoneflies develop through incomplete metamorphosis, passing from egg, to nymph, and then to adult. Stonefly nymphs are nearly all fast-water dwellers; there they may either feed on aquatic vegetation or prey on smaller nymphs and larvae. The type of feeding varies with the different species, as does the length of time spent in the nymphal stage. Most species take one year to develop from egg to adult, but some species may be in the stream for as long as three years. The stonefly nymph does not hatch in the water, but crawls out of the stream and then sheds its nymphal husk.

Nearly all species of adult stoneflies leave streamside immediately after hatching and fly to the surrounding brush, where they mate. The adult females return to the stream, usually three or four days later, to lay their eggs. The eggs may be dropped while the stonefly is flying, or they may be deposited by the female when she dips her abdomen in the water while flying or swims in the surface film to wash the eggs free (Illu. 3-3).

◼ 3-3. LIFE CYCLE OF THE STONEFLY

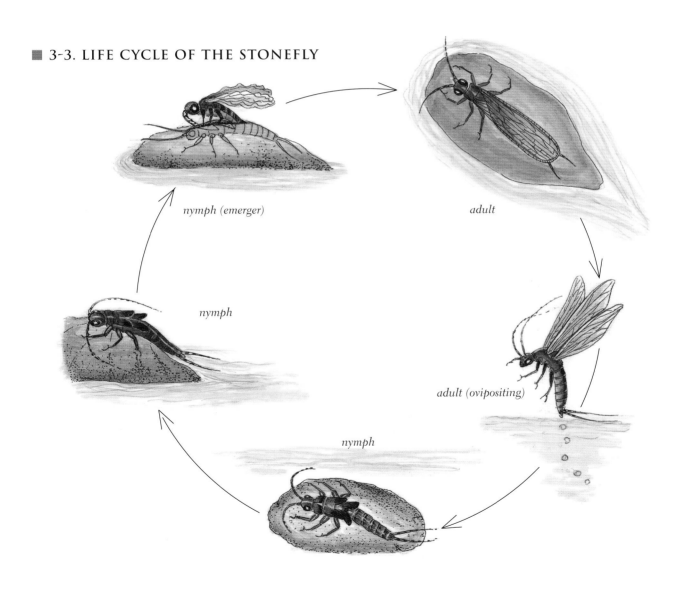

nymph (emerger)

adult

nymph

adult (ovipositing)

nymph

Life Cycle of the Midge (Diptera)

Midges undergo complete metamorphosis, changing from egg to larva to pupa and then to adult. Little is known about the details of their development, partly because of the large number of species and their diverse habits, and partly because the necessary research just hasn't been done to answer all of the questions concerning these tiny insects (Illu. 3-4).

Most midge larvae are found in the slow, silt-laden stretches of the stream, although a few species are found in fast water. They may be either herbivorous or carnivorous.

The pupa often develops in a cocoon attached to rocks or sticks on the stream bottom. Prior to emerging, the pupa ascends to the surface, where it

■ 3-4. LIFE CYCLE
OF THE MIDGE

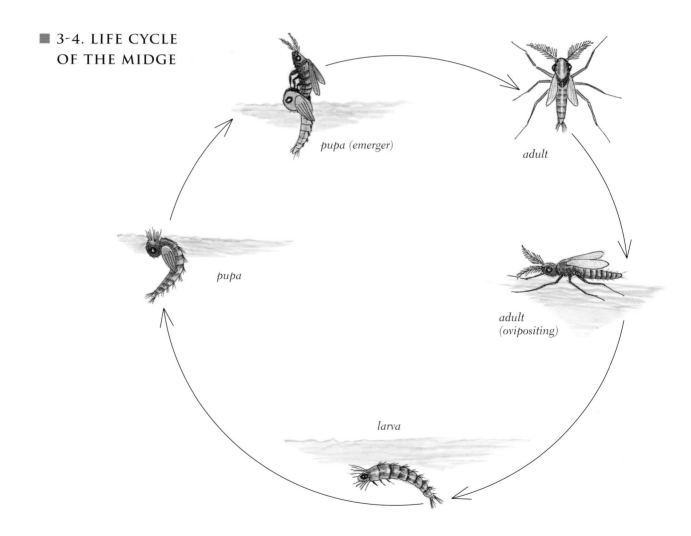

pupa (emerger)

adult

pupa

*adult
(ovipositing)*

larva

floats, suspended in the surface film by the gills surrounding its thorax, until the adult emerges.

The adult crawls out of the top of the pupal skin and flies low across the water. Occasionally, you will see small fish jumping clear of the water to capture the midge adults on the wing. The details of mating and egg laying are not clearly understood, and probably vary with the many species.

Nymphs and Larvae

MAYFLY NYMPH

With its incomplete metamorphosis, the mayfly has only a nymphal stage between the egg and the adult. When we tie and use a nymph, we are imitating this stage. Many of the standard wet-fly patterns are probably effective because they also imitate the nymphal stage.

The mayfly nymph has either two or three tails (most commonly three), a slim abdomen, and a large thorax with a hump on top, which is called the wing case. The wing case is the storage area for the developing wings (Illu. 3-5).

The tail is usually tied with hackle fibers or, as is becoming more common, with two or three heavy pieces of hair. The abdomen section is often tied with a quill body or floss to maintain the proper slim shape. The thorax area is commonly a dubbed section with a hackle wound through it to represent the legs. The wing case is most often represented by a section of a quill tied in at the rear of the thorax, laid forward over the dubbed section, and tied down at the head. A section of turkey quill is the traditional wing-case material, although any type of quill section may be used; a bunch of hair is utilized on some patterns and many synthetic materials such as Swiss Straw can be used.

Remember, your goal is to represent the insect; as long as you tie a slim body, a full thorax, and an imitative wing case—all of the right color and proportion—the material used is of no importance. We are not implying that you must have the insect in hand or an illustration to work from. You may be tying from a pattern, but you are not limited to using exactly the same materials.

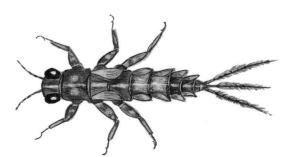

3-5. Mayfly nymph.

3-6. Caddisfly larva.

CADDISFLY LARVA

The caddisfly has no nymphal stage; the subaquatic stage that we are imitating is the larval stage. The larvae all have the same general appearance—they look like worms. They have short tails, which actually are hooks for securing themselves in their cases: highly segmented abdomens that are a little fatter than those of mayflies; and heads that are slightly larger and darker than their bodies. The free-swimming species looks similar, but without a case, of course.

Most caddisfly larva imitations leave off the tail. The body is sometimes floss with a wrap of fine wire or tinsel to provide segmentation, or the body may be made of a narrow strip of buckskin, latex, or even brass wire wound on the hook. The enlarged head may be thread wrapped to a diameter larger than the body, a dubbed area, or a few wraps of ostrich herl of the appropriate color (Illu. 3-6).

STONEFLY NYMPH

Incomplete metamorphosis, remember? This means that we are tying a nymphal imitation. The stonefly nymph spends its time clinging to the underside of rocks or debris on the stream bottom and becomes food to the trout when it is dislodged by heavy water or by other underwater disturbances.

The stonefly has two prominent tails, a highly segmented abdomen of fairly large diameter, a muscular thorax, and two wing cases that house the two pairs of developing wings (Illu. 3-7).

Two sections of turkey quill, tied in and separated, make a good tail. Any type of quill could be used in a like manner, but the insect has a mottled coloring and the turkey feathers match it nicely; on the other hand, so do pheasant, grouse tail, and many other feathers. Starting to get the picture? Only the end product is important, not the means. The heavy abdomen may be tied with several layers of floss, with a quill body wrapped over floss (to achieve the desired fullness), with latex strips or, as Don does it, with a rubber band. The thorax is nearly always dubbed, although chenille can be used, and a hackle is usually palmered through either. The wing case may be a quill section, latex, Swiss Straw, or hair.

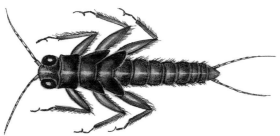

3-7. Stonefly nymph.

MIDGE LARVA

The order Diptera includes the crane flies as well as the midges, but gnats and other small members are of the most importance to the angler. Since they undergo complete metamorphosis, we will be imitating the larval stage. The midge larva's enlarged head and slim body closely resemble that of the caddisfly larva, but the midge larva has wing pads that hang on either side of the thorax area, giving it a slightly different profile (Illu. 3-8).

3-8. Midge larva.

Artificials are tied generally in the same way as the caddisfly larvae, although the thorax may be tied a little fuller to simulate the wing pads. The big difference is the smaller size of the midge larvae. Have you ever been standing in a stream, turned to say something to your buddy, and inhaled a half-zillion gnats? If so, you are acquainted with the midges. Midge larva imitations are commonly tied in sizes #22, #24, and #28. A quill body and a dubbed thorax are about all you need for this imitation.

Emergers

MAYFLY EMERGER

As the mayfly nymph starts its trip to the surface to emerge as an adult, it is basically the same shape as it was in the nymphal stage; however, the wing case is usually enlarged and somewhat darker than it was in the nymphal stage (Illu. 3-9). This trip may be repeated several times before the adult breaks through the surface film and emerges. During this period, the nymph is considerably more active than it was in its hiding place among the stream-bottom debris. This stage of increased activity is probably what we are imitating with a wet fly. Tied with soft hackle, the wet fly has a slim appearance in the water, and since it is most often worked upstream with some action imparted by the rod tip, it duplicates the increased activity of the soon-to-emerge nymph.

Patterns are usually tied with a small tail, a slim body of floss, quill, and a soft hackle that sweeps back along the body when wet. As you can see in Pattern 7, this is a reasonably good imitation of the insect.

3-9. Mayfly emerger.

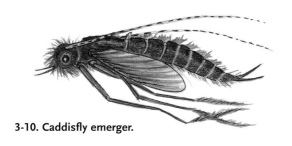

3-10. Caddisfly emerger.

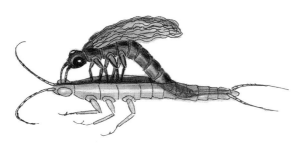

3-11. Stonefly emerger.

3-12. Midge emerger.

CADDISFLY EMERGER

The pupal stage of the caddisfly is spent in a case built of small pebbles, sticks, pieces of bark, and grass stems, which it built when it was a larva. Hatching time arrives when the pupa has been transformed into an adult within the pupal husk. It will swim to the surface and emerge; in a few species, the caddisfly will crawl out of the stream and emerge (Illu. 3-10).

The emerger stage may be imitated by a wet fly having an enlarged thorax region and perhaps wing pads on either side of the thorax. A standard dressed wet fly with a throat hackle is a reasonable imitation; this probably speaks for the success of this type of fly on occasion. The short, over-the-back wing often seen on a wet fly also imitates the emerging wing quite well.

STONEFLY EMERGER

Stonefly nymphs do not hatch in the water; they crawl out of the stream onto stones or branches near the water and escape from the nymphal skin as adults. It is doubtful that any of the wet flies are effective as emerger imitations of stoneflies, since this form of the insect is not normally available to the trout (Illu. 3-11).

MIDGE EMERGER

These tiny fellows undergo complete metamorphosis, so there is a pupal stage prior to the appearance of the adult. Most of the midge pupae have slim bodies, larger thoraxes, and wings held on either side of their thoraxes. There is a circle of filaments surrounding the head, and the body of the pupa hangs vertically in the water's film, suspended by these filaments (Illu. 3-12).

A few midge emerger imitations are tied in the following manner: a slim quill body is formed. Then a dubbed thorax is added. The dubbing is picked out or else a circle of hackle is wound at the head to represent the filaments.

As you can see, except for the mayfly nymph moving to the surface to hatch and the caddisfly pupa making the same type of journey, there is really not much for us to imitate in the emerger stage of an insect's life. Most successful wet flies are probably taken by the trout to be nymphs. The materials that you use to imitate the emerging mayfly nymph and the caddisfly pupa should be "soft" so that good motion is produced by its movement through the water. A slim body, enlarged thorax, and swollen, darkened wing cases are the most important points to remember.

Adults

MAYFLY ADULT

The newly emerged adult mayfly is known by the fisherman as a *dun*, while the entomologist calls this stage a *subimago*. During a "hatch," we try to duplicate this stage with our imitations.

3-13. Mayfly adult.

The mayfly dun ranges in length from 3 mm to 34 mm (#2 to #28 hooks) and has three tails (occasionally two), a very delicate abdomen, an enlarged thorax, four wings (two of which are quite small and normally are not imitated), and a small head. The mayfly dun's most distinguishing feature is its wings, which are carried upright like a sail. Any of the popular dry-fly patterns that have the wings in an upright position are imitating the mayfly dun (Illu. 3-13).

The tail may be made with a group of hackle fibers, a few pieces of hair tied in as a bunch, or two widely separated hairs as used on the Swisher-Richards "no-hackle" patterns. The slim body is often imitated by a quill wrapped on the hook, although dubbing has better floating qualities. Floss may be used in the same manner as quill. The thorax is usually tied of the same material as the body, and here is another advantage of dubbing: the thorax region can easily be enlarged by simply dubbing a little more heavily in that area. Wings may be represented by paired quill segments, hackle tips, a bunch of hair, polypropylene fibers, or rolled feathers. Color and size are critical for a successful imitation, but the type of body construction, type of wing, and method of tying the tail are not important as long as a good imitation of the adult insect is the result.

After leaving the stream, the dun molts again. The fisherman calls this stage a *spinner*; the scientist uses the term *imago*. Following this final molt, the insect is more brightly colored, with a slimmer, more delicate appearance and a longer tail. The mayflies return to the water to mate, and as copulation is completed and the eggs are deposited, the insects fall onto the water and lie expired in the surface film with their wings outstretched (spent).

An artificial spinner is tied in much the same way as the dun imitation is, except for the following: colors may be brighter, a longer hook is used to represent the longer body, the tails are longer, and the wings are tied so they lie perpendicular to the sides of the thorax. Hackle tips are most commonly used for the wings, although hair and shaped polypropylene yarn are very effective.

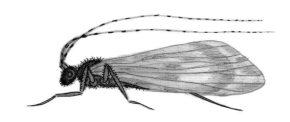

3-14. Caddisfly adult.

CADDISFLY ADULT

The caddisfly adult has no tail, has a fairly heavy body, and carries its wings over its back in an inverted "V". Although the adult has no tail, it does carry its legs out behind it when at rest, and since a tail on our fly serves the important mechanical function of supporting the heaviest part of the hook (the bend), patterns are usually tied with a tail. The body can be made of any of the materials that we have previously mentioned (and many that weren't), but dubbing is hard to beat, not only because of its excellent floating properties, but because of the subtle shade that can be obtained by mixing different colors. The wing is most often imitated by a bunch of hair tied in over the back (Illu. 3-14).

STONEFLY ADULT

The stonefly adult crawls out of the water to hatch on a nearby stick or stone. The frequent appearance of stoneflies on the water may be the result of a gust of wind, or perhaps just plain clumsiness; they fell in (as I do sometimes). Two tails, a heavy body, a muscular thorax, and wings carried in a flat position over the back are the most recognizable characteristics of the stonefly adult. Many of the caddisfly imitations may be taken by the trout to be stoneflies, since their shape is much the same. The stonefly, however, is usually tied on a longer hook than a caddisfly of the same size (Illu. 3-15).

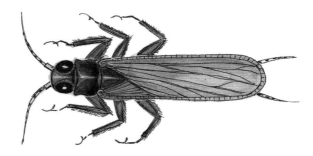

3-15. Stonefly adult.

MIDGE ADULT

Adult midges are very hard to categorize with a simple description as they are so numerous and varied. The basic point is that they are generally very small and mosquitolike. They most often carry their wings in a spent position, although a flat V shape is not uncommon.

Because of the midge's small size, a detailed imitation is extremely difficult to tie: fortunately, it doesn't seem to be required. Most patterns are tied using just a tail, a dubbed body, and a hackle. Ostrich herl is also a good choice for a body material; since the hooks used are quite small, a hackle feather may not be required as the fibers of herl can float the fly nicely (Illu. 3-16).

We have intentionally left out any reference to the hackle feathers used for tying the adult stages. Since the hackle feather is the prime support for the fly, it must be of good quality. Choose a hackle feather first of all by color; it must be right for the insect that you are imitating. It must be of the right size, both to look right to you and to support the fly properly. Its quality must be sufficient to float the fly: stiff, resilient fibers, long enough to tie easily, with a good sheen. You will find that your quest for good hackle feathers in a wide range of colors will go a long way toward keeping your local fly shop proprietors in the style to which they would like to become accustomed.

There they are—the most important insects to the fisherman and how we go about imitating them. Basically, fly-tying is just having knowledge of the materials available to you and perfecting the skill to use those materials. The knowledge of the insects is readily available in many fine books; the common patterns are effective because they are representative of the actual insects. Keep in mind that you are trying to duplicate the insect and not the pattern, and learn to keep your mind open for logical, workable substitutions of materials and methods. A wing is a wing regardless of the method used to tie it.

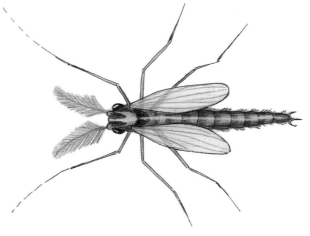

3-16. Midge adult.

OTHER FLIES: STREAMERS, TERRESTRIALS AND ATTRACTORS

Streamers

Most of the modern streamer flies are tied as baitfish imitations and might be defined as flies that use the wing as the bulk and mass of the body material. Generally, the material wound on the hook shank is quite sparse, commonly just a layer of floss or tinsel, which serves to represent the shiny belly of a minnow. Wing material is then tied in at the head of the fly so that it will lie on top of the hook to form the main body shape. Often, several colors of material are tied in to form layers of color that when wet will suggest the coloring of a particular type of small fish. An example would be an imitation of a small rainbow trout tied in this manner: silver tinsel wound on the hook shank to represent the shiny belly, pink hair or marabou tied in on top of the hook, with yellow above that to represent the main body color, and green hair or marabou or, perhaps, peacock on top to imitate the dark dorsal area. See Patterns 15, 16, 17, and 18 for examples of streamers. Illu. 4-1 shows one example.

The materials used for streamers are usually chosen for their ability to move in the water, which imitates the swimming action of a minnow.

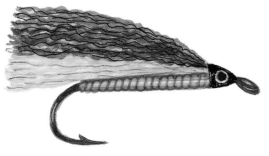

4-1. A marabou streamer.

Soft hackle, bucktail, marabou, and peacock are commonly used along with any number of synthetic materials.

The hooks used for streamers are generally long-shanked (3X to 6X), of heavy wire (2X stout), and are often ring-eyed. The added length is needed to represent the body length of the minnow, the extra stout wire aids in getting the imitation down, and the ring eye gives the streamer a more realistic movement as it is worked in and out of the pockets and eddies of the stream.

Terrestrials

Terrestrials are forms of insect life that are not normally part of the aquatic scene. Ants, grasshoppers, beetles, swarming termites, and any other land-based insects that find themselves in the water are examples.

Terrestrials are nearly always tied as dry flies: they may be tied using the same materials and techniques that we discussed earlier. The number of patterns to work from is greatly reduced though, and the tyer must be more inventive. Grasshoppers seem to be a preferred trout food, and the ability to tie a good "hopper" imitation is important. Beetles and ants are very effective at times and should be a part of any tyer's repertoire. Just as when tying aquatic imitations, the tyers of terrestrials should be observant while on the stream so that when they return to the tying table they know what they need to have ready for the next trip. The terrestrials available to the trout depend on the time of the year and many local influences, so close observation is important.

4-2. A dry-fly attractor.

Attractors

Attractor flies are those that generally appeal to some instinct other than hunger. They are not a realistic imitation of any particular creature and often have very bright colors. A good example is the Royal Coachman; there isn't any insect that looks like this red, green, and white fly, and yet this pattern has historically been the single most popular fly. Why do trout take it? No one is sure, but the trout may be striking out of curiosity, playfulness, or maybe he's *really* hungry and it looks like something that may be edible. In the case of attractor-type streamers, territorial possession is perhaps the most logical reason for the trout's interest, although the other instincts mentioned may be involved on occasion. Whatever the reasons, attractors do work at times. The only differences between tying attractors and tying the flies that we have already discussed are the colors and arrangement of materials; no special techniques are required. Patterns 21 through 24 are examples of attractors. Illu. 4-2 shows one, a dry-fly attractor (Pattern 22).

■ BEFORE YOU BEGIN

Fly-Tying Classes

IT IS POSSIBLE TO LEARN TO TIE WITHOUT ATTENDING A fly-tying class. This manual is meant to make that easier, but we know that even though we have duplicated our classroom presentation as closely as possible, we could teach you more and you would learn faster if we were watching over your shoulder.

Classes are offered at many schools, in community recreation programs, by sportsmen's clubs, and by many tackle shops. Ferret one out and enroll. Don't feel that just because you can already tie, there is nothing to learn or that you will have to start all over. A good instructor will not change your basic methods (if they are sound) although he or she will, in all likelihood, show you some other ways of achieving the same result and leave it to you to determine which works best for you. Classes are kept small so the students can receive individual attention. As a result, the instructor can introduce you to the more advanced techniques, which the true beginner in the class won't get to see. Do get into a class if at all possible and, above all, keep an open mind as to what is taught. We all tie differently (even Don and I), but that doesn't mean that someone is doing it wrong. The only pitfall to avoid is the instructor (or book) that insists on teaching THE way to tie.

Fly-Tying Kits

THE PRICE OF INDIVIDUAL DECENT-QUALITY TYING TOOLS
runs from around $60 to $100 as of this writing. There is no way—repeat
NO WAY—that a kit can sell for much less without being junk.

Most fly shops and mail order suppliers sell kits for around $80 to $100
that would cost much more if sold as individual items at retail prices. The
theory is simple. If you never start tying or if you start with poor equipment
and give up in frustration, you aren't going to buy any more tying materials,
right? Besides, when you come in to get that spool of thread, you just might
fall in love with that new graphite rod, or reel, or vest, or.... It's just smart
business to sell you a good kit.

In judging the quality of a kit, look first at the tools; if they are of good
quality, you can be reasonably sure that the kit is a good one because the
merchant has most of the cost represented there. The materials are relatively
inexpensive because of the merchant's volume buying; materials are but a
small part of expenses, so the merchant can afford to be generous with them.

Now that you have found a kit that contains good tools and a nice variety
of materials, meeting the criteria we have outlined, you are ready to tie anything, right? Wrong. The variety of materials used in fly-tying is unlimited,
and a kit that included some of *everything* would have to be transported
home in a truck. If it included all colors of everything, a boxcar wouldn't be
adequate. A good kit will contain some of the most often used materials so
that the beginner can learn to handle these materials. That's the best that the
kit assembler can do.

SPECIFIC PROBLEMS AND THEIR SOLUTIONS

This chapter is intended as a reference, should you have difficulty with a particular step in the tying process. We have listed the most common problems and their solutions under two headings: "Problems with Tools" and "Problems with Parts of the Fly." To avoid cross-referencing between problems that have the same solution, we have given the solution with each problem so that you will not have to spend a lot of time looking for the answer to your difficulty.

Problems with Tools

VISE

Hook slips. The most likely problem is that the vise is improperly adjusted; check the manufacturer's instructions for proper adjustment. The same difficulty may be experienced if you have your bobbin tension set too tight; remove the spool of thread and spread the legs of the bobbin apart slightly.

Hook breaks. You may have gotten a batch of bad hooks; check each one as you mount it in the vise by tweaking the eye with your fingernail. It should spring back to shape. If the hooks seem to be good, you may be setting the hook back too far in the vise jaws and destroying the temper of the steel; only the bend of the hook should be clamped in the vise.

HACKLE PLIERS

Pliers cut hackle. There is a sharp edge on the pliers; work a doubled piece of fine emery paper between the closed jaws to smooth them, or put shrink tubing over the jaws.

Pliers slip. Either the hackle pliers don't have enough tension or the jaws are glazed (if you are using shrink tubing on the jaws). To increase the tension, unhook the jaws and spread the pliers' legs apart; to eliminate slipping due to glazing, rough up the tubing with emery paper.

SCISSORS

Scissors aren't cutting. Make sure that the joint where the two blades are fastened together is tight; nearly all good-quality scissors have a screw that secures the blades together. Perhaps the scissors need sharpening; check with your barber or beautician to see where they get theirs done. For temporary sharpening, you may be able to get by with cutting a piece of fine emery paper a few times. If the scissors seem to be tight and sharp, you have probably sprung the jaws; the only solution is to buy a new pair, but keep the old ones for cutting wire, rubber, and other tough things so that the new pair won't suffer the same fate.

BOBBIN

Bobbin cuts thread. The bobbin has a rough edge at the end of the tube. To remedy, cut a small, triangular piece of emery paper, roll it into a cone, and polish the inside of the tip.

Bobbin is slipping. The bobbin tension is set too loose; remove the spool of thread and bend the legs of the bobbin toward each other. For a slight increase in tension, slip a couple of wraps of thread from the end of the spool onto one of the legs of the bobbin.

Thread is breaking. The thread tension is set too tight; remove the spool of thread and spread the legs of the bobbin apart a small amount.

Threading problems. The quickest and easiest way to thread the bobbin is to pull off 5" or 6" of thread, start the thread into the end of the tube and then suck on the other end of the tube to pull the thread through. You can also buy a bobbin threader to solve the problem.

Problems with Parts of the Fly

TAIL

Tail rolls around the hook as it is tied in. After tying the butts of the tailing material down, hold the tail slightly toward you as you wrap to the back of the hook and allow the thread to carry the tailing material to the top center of the hook shank.

Tail is tipped down. The angle of the tail is determined by how far you wrap back on the tailing material; if you wrap too far back, you will tip the tail down as you start around the bend of the hook.

RIBBING

Ribbing breaks. If the problem is with tinsel, there is probably a kink in the tinsel; be certain that the tinsel is smooth before tying it in. A quill that is being used for ribbing material will break if you try to wrap it too tightly. It might also be too dry; soak it for a few minutes in water and it will soften.

BODY

Quill breaks. A quill being used for a body must be handled gently. If you are not applying too much pressure and are still experiencing breaking, the quill may be dry; all stripped quill will soften if soaked in water.

Floss is fraying. Fraying is the most common problem encountered when using floss, and the problem is increased if your hands are rough. Keep a bottle or tube of hand lotion on the bench for use when your hands are rough. Keeping the floss wet when you are wrapping it will help to alleviate the problem and also will result in a smoother fly body.

Floss is separating. Most of the floss used for fly-tying is made of four strands, and the strands have a tendency to separate as the floss is wrapped. Keeping the floss wet will help to keep the strands together, and holding the floss close to the hook shank assists in overcoming the problem.

Dubbing is separating from the thread. You are probably either trying to dub too long a piece of thread at one time or trying to put too much fur on the thread; you should dub the thread rather sparsely and only dub 1" or 2" of thread at a time. If a longer piece is needed, you should dub a section, wrap it, dub another section, and so on, until the desired length of body is obtained.

Body is not tapered. Trying to dub too heavily may be the problem; the thread should be dubbed rather lightly. Another common problem is wrapping all of one piece of dubbing on the hook before dubbing the next section of thread. When you dub a small section of thread, you will notice that the dubbing is thicker in the center of the dubbed area and thinner at each end; if you will stop winding when this taper is still above the hook shank and then dub the next section, the two tapers will overlap and give you a section of dubbing of equal diameter for its full length.

Spun hair is not flaring properly. This is most often the result of having the thread wrapped under the area where you intend to spin the hair; the hook shank needs to be bare at this point. Attempting to spin too much hair at one time will result in the same problem.

Spun hair is not smooth after trimming. The secret of a perfectly smooth body after trimming it to shape is to singe it; hold a match flame above the body and use the underside of the flame to smooth the body. You can actually shape the trimmed body by this method, and it also seals the ends of the trimmed hair and makes the fly more buoyant.

Rubber body is too bulky or too thin. The shape of a wrapped rubber body (of either heavy latex or rubber band) is determined by the amount of tension that is applied during the wrapping process. When starting the wrap, stretch the material tightly, and as you wrap the material around the hook shank, loosen the tension slightly with each wrap. This allows the material to thicken with each wrap and will produce a nicely tapered body.

WING CASE

Wing case is rolling off top of hook. You must use the soft-loop technique to tie in the wing case, so that it will remain in position as the thread is tightened. Use at least two soft loops to anchor the material before continuing with normal wrapping. See Pattern 1, steps 5, 10, and 26, for a description of the soft-loop technique.

Wing case is splitting. The wing case material is probably too wide if you are having problems with it splitting; the width of the wing case should be about one-fourth of the length of the hook shank. If you are using a quill section for the wing case, do not trim the top of a palmered hackle before bringing the wing case forward, as the stiff hackle fibers that are left will puncture the wing case material and cause splitting.

WINGS

Quill wing is splitting. This problem is normally the result of using too wide a piece of quill or of not holding the wing firmly in place during the tying-in step; each quill section should have a width equal to about one-fourth of the length of the hook shank, and you must make at least two "soft loops" to anchor the wing before continuing the wrapping process.

Quill wing is rolling. Holding the wings firmly in place until they are anchored with at least two "soft loops" will solve this problem; a base of thread on the hook shank where the wing is to be mounted will also help.

Rolled wing is rolling off the top of the hook. This problem is most commonly caused by not holding the wing firmly in place while using the soft loop for the tie-in; you must have at least two wraps using the soft loop before letting go of the wing material to continue the wrapping.

Hackle-tip wing is twisting. Often the lower part of a hackle stem is oval in cross section and the hackle will tend to twist as it is tied in. Softening the tip by gently chewing it is the most expedient solution; if you select the hackle tip from nearer the tip of a larger feather, the stem is more likely to be round.

Hair wing has uneven tips. Using a hair stacker or its equivalent is the best solution to this difficulty.

Hair wing is rolling. This is the most difficult problem when tying a hair wing; you must be certain that you have at least three wraps ("soft loops") before letting go of the winging material.

Hair wing is pulling out. To mount the wing so that it will stay firmly in place, make sure that you have a layer of tying thread under the area where the wing will be tied in, and after tying it in put a couple drops of head cement on the windings.

HACKLE

Hackle is breaking. If the hackle is breaking at the end of the hackle pliers, the problem is normally with the tool; there is a sharp edge that is cutting the hackle. If the stem is breaking at the point where it is tied in, the cause is probably that the hackle is too dry; steaming it over a tea kettle will soften the stem without harming the hackle fibers. If the hackle is breaking somewhere between the hackle pliers and the tie-in point, you have a bad neck; the hackle has been damaged by either disease or insects. Occasionally you can salvage some hackles by steaming them to soften the stems and wrapping them very carefully.

Hackle doesn't flare properly. The hackle feathers on some necks have very pronounced oval stems and are very difficult to wrap edgewise. You can steam the neck to soften the stems, but once in a while you will get a neck that you just can't use for hackling because of this problem.

Hackle pulls out. This is easily remedied by stripping a slightly longer section of the hackle butt, tying the stem in behind the wing, and then anchoring it again in front of the wing. This locks the stem around the lump at the base of the wing.

HEAD

Hackle tips unintentionally tied down. Usually this problem started when you mounted the wing. You set it too far toward the eye of the hook, and by the time you wound the hackle there just wasn't room for the head; check the proportion illustration shown on page 50 for the proper wing position. If you had room for the head and are still experiencing this problem, you are not keeping the hackle back out of the way with your left hand while forming the head; if you just can't get the knack of this technique you might consider using hackle guards.

PROPORTIONS OF MATERIALS TO HOOKS FOR VARIOUS FLIES

Here is a page of diagrams to show the proportions of materials to hooks for various types of fly. This will be a handy reference page when you start tying flies. In the upper left is a diagram showing the hand position for holding the bobbin.

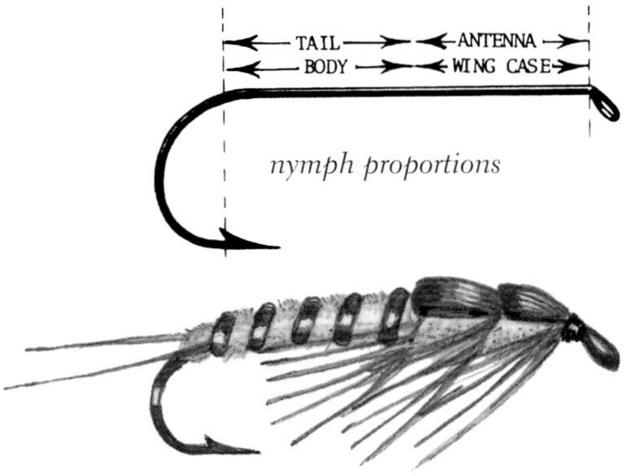

TAIL — ANTENNA
BODY — WING CASE

nymph proportions

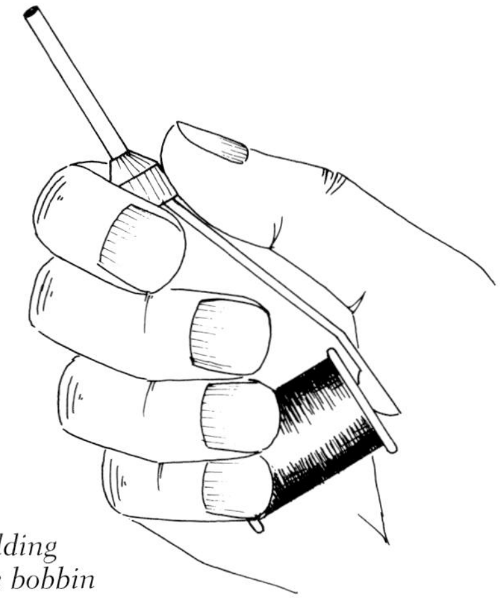

holding the bobbin

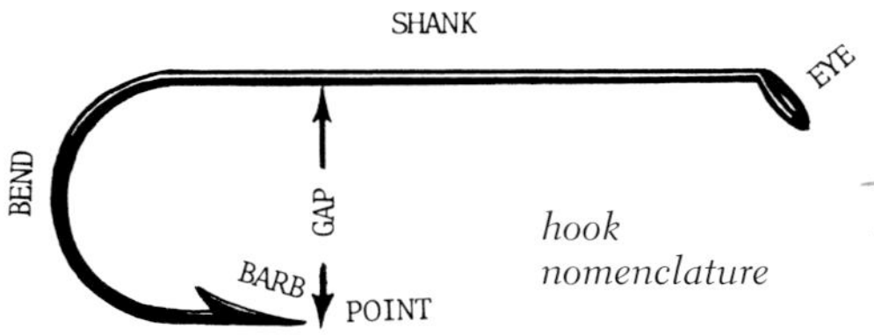

HACKLE 1½ x GAP

WING
TAIL
GAP

dry-fly proportions

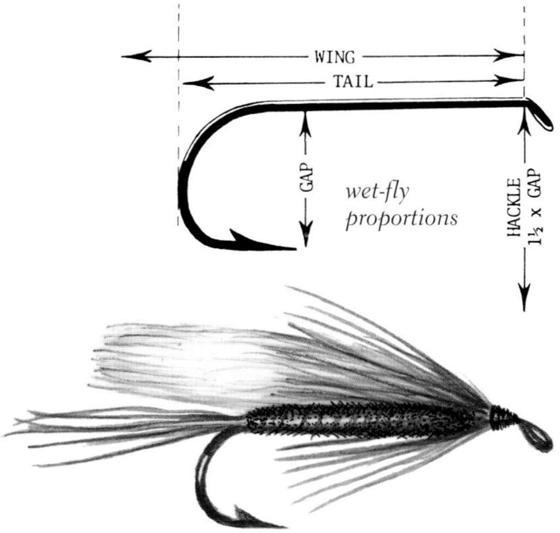

SHANK
EYE
BEND
GAP
BARB
POINT

hook nomenclature

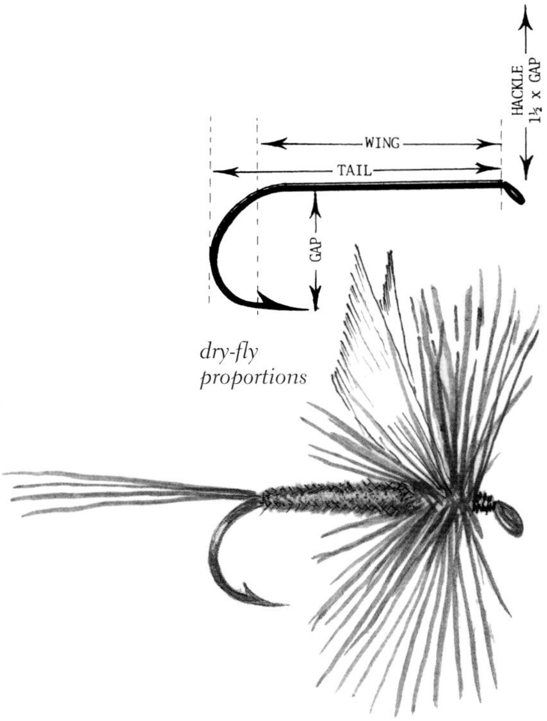

WING
TAIL
GAP
HACKLE 1½ x GAP

wet-fly proportions

TAIL — THROAT HACKLE
WING

streamer proportions

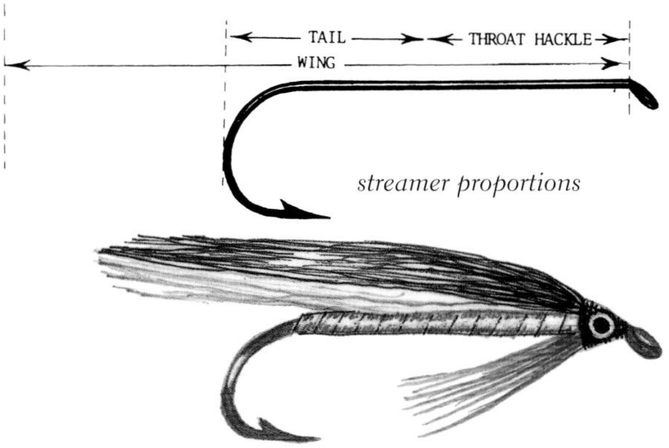

PATTERNS

SIMPLE

CADDISFLY LARVA

THE FIRST FLY THAT WE ARE GOING TO HAVE YOU TIE is a simple caddisfly (Trichoptera) larva imitation. Caddisfly larvae vary greatly in size, from about the size of a #10 hook to smaller than a #20 and, of course, the imitation should be tied on a hook that will give the correct size for the natural fly that you are trying to imitate. For the purpose of instruction, however, we suggest that you begin tying on a #10 or #12 hook. Since caddisfly larvae are found near the bottom of the stream, you should use a wet-fly hook.

In our illustrations, the fly is tied with a wool body, ribbed with fine brass wire; the thorax area is made of peacock feather. For the body you could substitute dubbing, ostrich herl, peacock feather, or any other material that would give the desired fuzzy appearance. The ribbing might be thread, tinsel, or a quill. Dubbing or ostrich would be good alternatives for the thorax area. The most common colors are olive, gray, white, and tan, but certainly your choice should depend on the insects that are present in the streams where you fish.

Pay particular attention to the technique shown in steps 5, 10, and 26—the soft-loop technique. This is the most important technique in all of fly-tying. The soft loop is used to attach all material to the hook and will become critically important in some of the later patterns.

1. Start wrapping two eyewidths back from the eye. The thread should be on the near side of the hook.

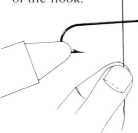

2. Wrap over the top of the hook (away from you) to a point one eyewidth back from the eye.

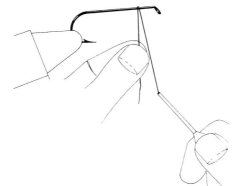

3. Wrap the thread back over itself to the original starting point.

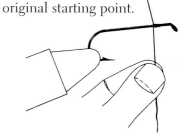

4. Hold a 4" piece of fine brass wire in your left hand as shown.

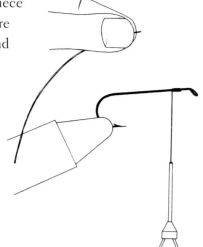

5. Hold the wire on top of the hook shank and bring the thread up between your thumb and the hook; as the thread is brought down on the other side of the hook, hold the thread in a "soft loop."

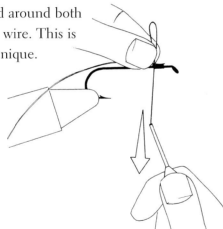

6. Pull down on the bobbin to tighten the thread around both the hook and the wire. This is the soft-loop technique.

7. Holding the wire with your left hand so that it stays on the top of the hook shank, start wrapping the thread to the rear of the hook.

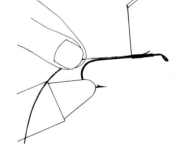

8. Stop the wraps at a point directly opposite the barb of the hook.

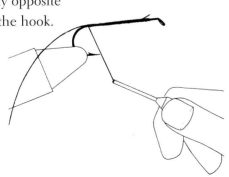

9. Wrap the thread forward to the original tie-in point and trim off the excess wire.

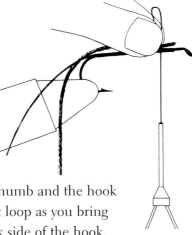

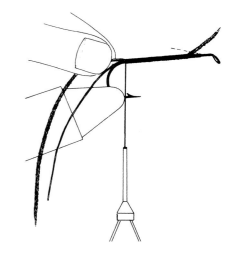

10. Hold a 5" piece of wool yarn on the top of the hook shank with the left hand. Pinching both the yarn and the hook, bring the thread up between the thumb and the hook and hold the thread in a soft loop as you bring the thread down on the back side of the hook. Pull down on the bobbin to tighten the thread around the hook and yarn; repeat three times to anchor the end of the yam.

11. Wrap back to a point opposite the barb of the hook while holding the yarn on the top of the hook shank. Trim off the short end of the wool at the tie-in point.

12. Wrap the thread forward to the tie-in point and start wrapping the wool forward by wrapping away from yourself with your right hand.

13. Pass the yarn to your left hand under the hook. Your left hand stays in this position.

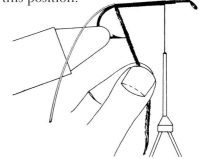

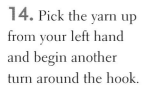

14. Pick the yarn up from your left hand and begin another turn around the hook.

15. Pass the yarn to your left hand under the hook.

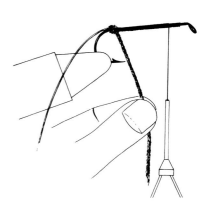

16. Pick the yarn up with your right hand and begin another wrap.

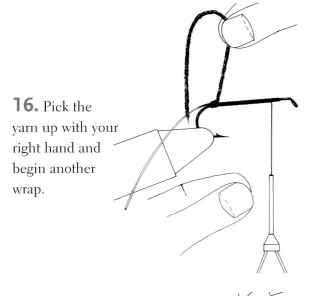

17. Note that your left hand stays under the hook at all times and that your right hand does the actual wrapping.

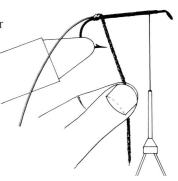

18. Continue wrapping in this manner until the original tie-in point is reached.

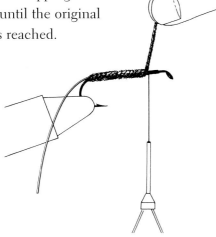

19. Hold the yarn as shown with your right hand; pick up the bobbin with your left hand and pass it over the top of the hook and allow it to drop on the other side. Continue wrapping the thread over the yarn using this method for three turns.

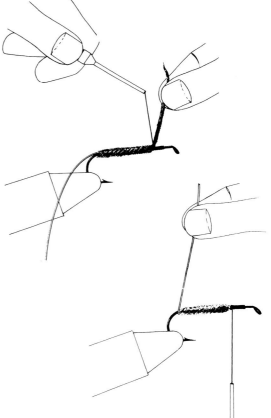

20. Hold the end of the yarn up with your left hand and cut off the excess.

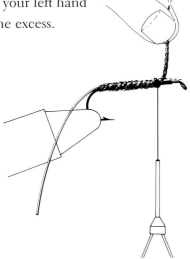

21. Begin wrapping the wire forward (away from you, over the top) with your right hand.

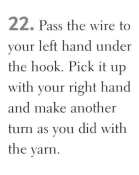

22. Pass the wire to your left hand under the hook. Pick it up with your right hand and make another turn as you did with the yarn.

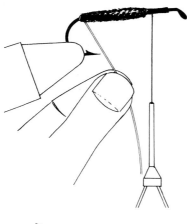

23. Wrap the wire forward in a spiral as illustrated to the tie-in point.

24. Hold the wire in your right hand and tie down the wire by wrapping the thread over it with your left hand. Remember, you will have to drop the bobbin during each wrap. Make at least three wraps over the wire.

25. Trim off the end of the wire with your heavy scissors.

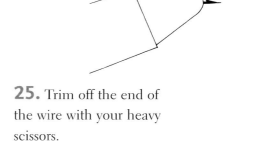

26. Select two peacock herl and hold them on top of the hook shank. Bring the thread up between the hook and your thumb and hold the thread in a soft loop as you bring the thread down the back side of the hook.

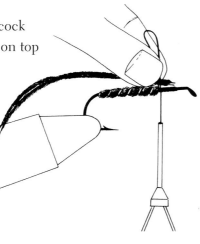

27. Tighten the loop on the hook and the peacock herl and then wrap the thread forward to a point one eye-width back of the eye.

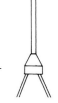

28. Start wrapping the peacock herl toward the eye of the hook with your right hand.

29. Pass the herl to your left hand under the hook.

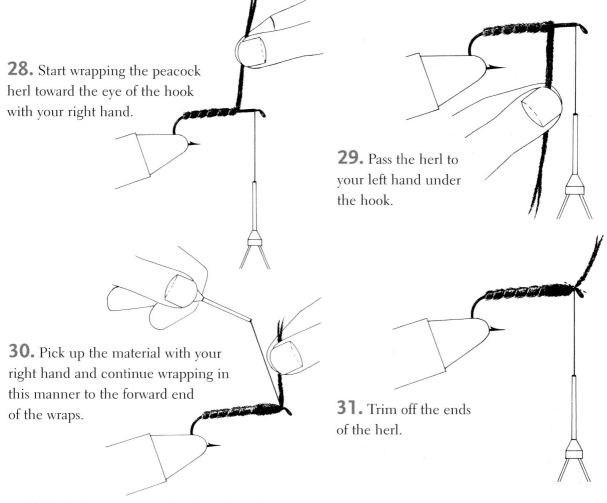

30. Pick up the material with your right hand and continue wrapping in this manner to the forward end of the wraps.

31. Trim off the ends of the herl.

Hold the herl in your right hand and tie the herl down by passing the bobbin over the top, dropping it, picking it up, and passing it over the top again. Make at least four wraps to anchor the ends of the herl.

32 to 38. Using the steps illustrated, tie the half-hitch three times to finish the head of the fly. For clarity, only tying off the head is shown in Steps 32 through 38; however, the other body materials are actually on the hook, as in Step 31.

32.

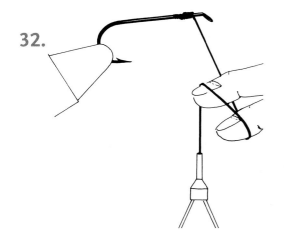

33.

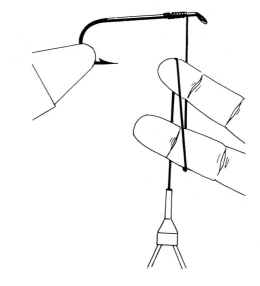

34.

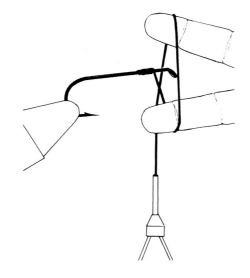

35.

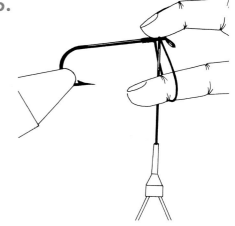

36.

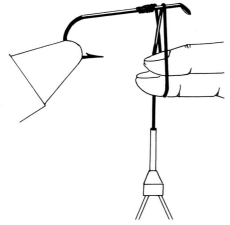

37.

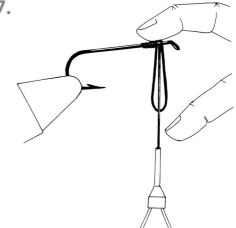

38.

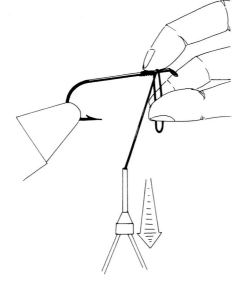

39. The finished fly.

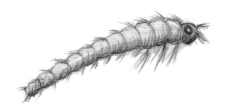

PATTERN
2

MIDGE
LARVA

THIS FLY IS AN ADAPTATION OF A PATTERN originated by Mr. Ed Marsh to imitate the caddisfly larva found in the South Platte River in Colorado. We have adapted it for a midge larva imitation and it has worked for us very successfully. You'll remember from the chapter on insects that the caddisfly larva and the midge larva are very similar in appearance; size is the primary difference. Later you will want to tie this fly in sizes down to #24, but for now use a #12 to give yourself a chance to gain the necessary dexterity before tackling the little ones. Since the imitation will be fished near the bottom, you should use a wet- fly hook.

We show this pattern tied with a white floss body, gold wire ribbing, a soft hair throat, and a dubbed thorax to match the body color. The desired body color is obtained by simply changing the color of the tying thread; the white floss will become translucent when wet and the thread color will show through as a dark streak. Black thread will give a nice blue dun color, green will come through as a delicate olive, and orange will produce a rusty tan. Thin latex rubber body material will give much the same result. The throat could be tied using hackle fibers or any soft hair or feather. We often tie this with no throat or dubbing; instead, we use ostrich herl of a color that matches the body for the entire thorax.

The main learning objective in this pattern is the dubbing process. Take particular care with it. Use a soft fur for the dubbing as it is easier to learn with it; rabbit, muskrat, or mink would be good choices. Try spinning the dubbing directly onto the tying thread first; if you have trouble that way, wet your fingers and try again. As a last resort, try waxing the portion of the thread that you are going to dub. If you still have trouble, you are probably trying to spin too much fur at a time.

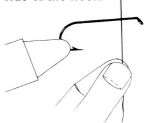

1. Start wrapping two eyewidths back from the eye. The thread should be on the near side of the hook.

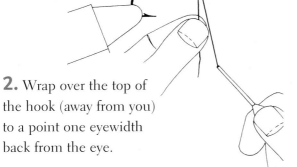

2. Wrap over the top of the hook (away from you) to a point one eyewidth back from the eye.

3. Wrap the thread back over itself to the original starting point.

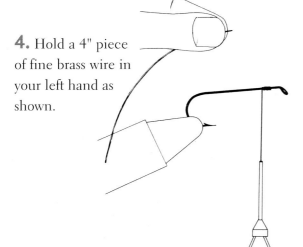

4. Hold a 4" piece of fine brass wire in your left hand as shown.

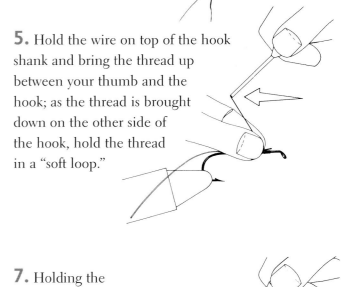

5. Hold the wire on top of the hook shank and bring the thread up between your thumb and the hook; as the thread is brought down on the other side of the hook, hold the thread in a "soft loop."

6. Pull down on the bobbin to tighten the thread around both the hook and the wire. This is the soft-loop technique.

7. Holding the wire with your left hand so that it stays on the top of the hook shank, start wrapping the thread to the rear of the hook.

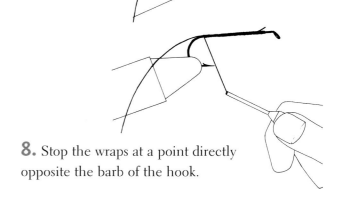

8. Stop the wraps at a point directly opposite the barb of the hook.

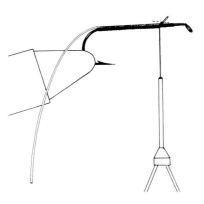

9. Wrap the thread forward to the original tie-in point and trim off the excess wire.

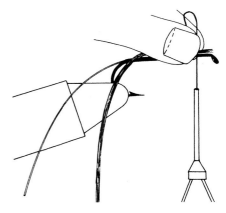

10. Hold a 5" piece of floss on the top of the hook shank with the left hand. Pinching both the floss and the hook, bring the thread up between the thumb and the hook and hold the thread in a soft loop as you bring the thread down on the back side of the hook. Pull down on the bobbin to tighten the thread around the hook and floss. Repeat three times to anchor the end of the floss.

11. Wrap the thread to a point opposite the barb of the hook; trim off the short end of the floss at the front of the hook. Wind the thread forward to the original tie-in point.

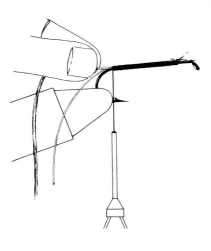

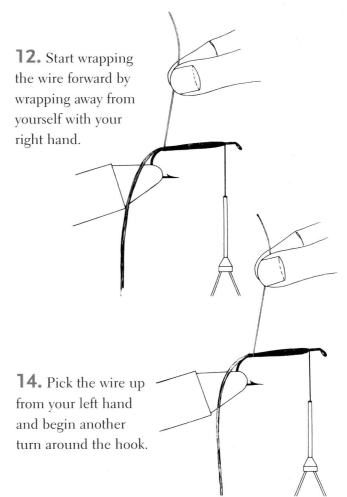

12. Start wrapping the wire forward by wrapping away from yourself with your right hand.

13. Pass the wire to your left hand under the hook. Your left hand stays in this position.

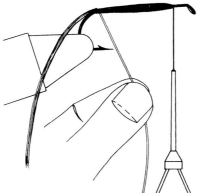

14. Pick the wire up from your left hand and begin another turn around the hook.

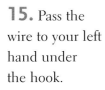

15. Pass the wire to your left hand under the hook.

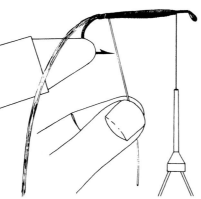

16. Continue wrapping in the same manner, spiraling the wire as shown to the front of the thread wraps. Tie down the wire and trim off the excess.

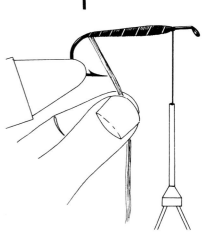

17. Begin wrapping the floss forward (away from you, over the top) with your right hand.

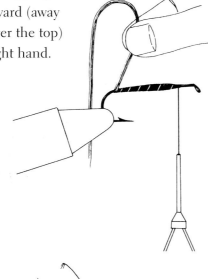

18. Pass the floss to your left hand under the hook. Pick it up with your right hand and make another turn as you did with the yarn. When wrapping floss keep your fingers close to the hook shank to prevent separation of the strands.

19. Wrap in this manner to the front of the thread wraps and tie the floss down.

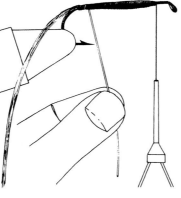

20. Trim off the excess floss.

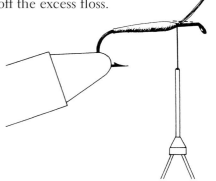

21. Invert the hook in the vise and measure a bunch of hair or hackle fibers as shown.

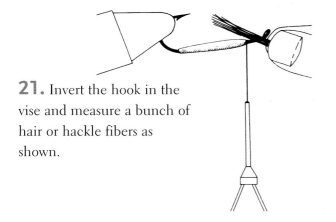

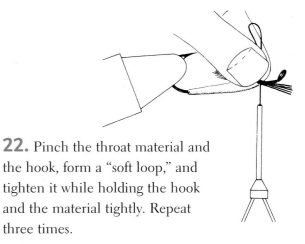

22. Pinch the throat material and the hook, form a "soft loop," and tighten it while holding the hook and the material tightly. Repeat three times.

23. Trim off the excess throat material as shown.

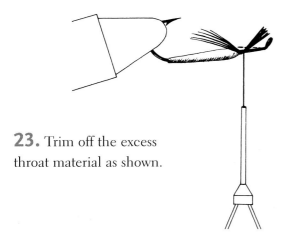

24. Cut a patch of dubbing fur from the hide and pull out the guard (coarse) hairs.

25. Place the hook upright in the vise. Hold the thread taut and place a small patch of dubbing against the thread.

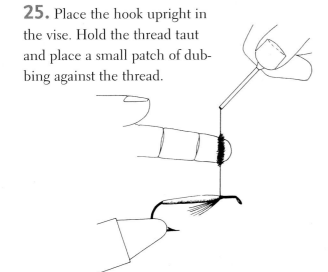

26. Close your thumb and forefinger so that the dubbing and the thread are between them.

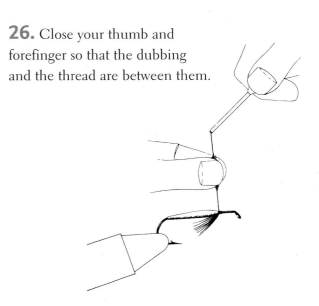

27. Roll the thumb and finger away from each other to "spin" the fur onto the thread; repeat until the thread and dubbing form a "yarn." The spinning motion must be in only one direction, not back and forth.

28. Slide the dubbing down the thread to the hook shank.

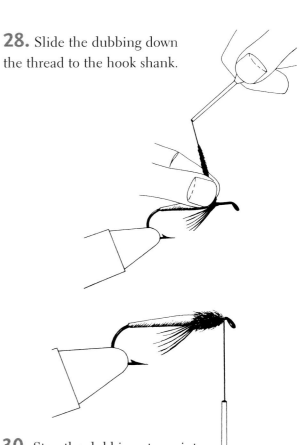

29. Start wrapping the dubbing forward towards the eye of the hook.

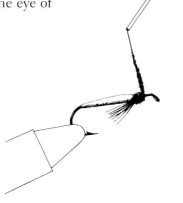

30. Stop the dubbing at a point one eyewidth back from the eye.

31 to 37. Using the steps illustrated, tie the half-hitch three times to form the head of the fly. For clarity, only tying off the head is shown in Steps 31 through 37; however, the other body materials are actually on the hook, as in Step 30.

31.

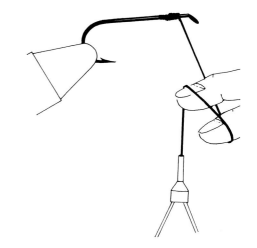

32.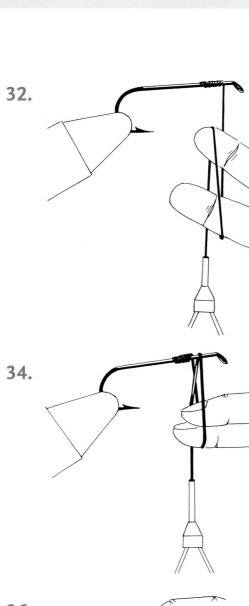

33.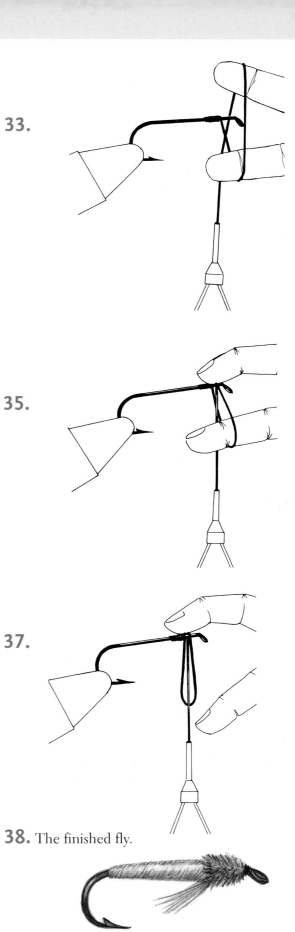

34.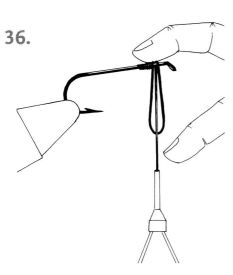

35.

36.

37.

38. The finished fly.

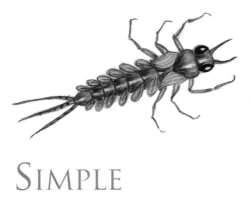

SIMPLE

MAYFLY NYMPH

THIS IS A SIMPLE MAYFLY (EMPHEMEROPTERA) NYMPH IMITATION. Since you are going to fish it deep, you should tie it on a wet-fly hook. Some of the Ephemeroptera nymphs are rather long-bodied, and for these you will want to use a 1X or 2X long hook.

We show the tail as soft hackle fibers, but soft hair or soft body-feather fibers would work equally well. The dubbing can be any soft underfur such as rabbit, mink, fox, muskrat, or one of the synthetics. The throat is traditionally tied of the same material as the tail. The wing case that we show is cut from a small mallard body feather that has been lacquered with head cement, but a piece of lacquered turkey quill or pheasant tail, or many other materials could be used.

When dubbing for a body, you generally won't be able to dub a section of thread long enough to wrap the whole body. A good method is to dub a relatively short section, wrap until all but ½" or so is on the hook, and then dub another section. The advantage of this method is that when you spin the dubbing, it will be thicker in the center of the section and taper at each end. By dubbing another section before the first is completely wrapped, the two tapered ends will overlap and the junction of the two sections will be the same diameter as the center area.

1. Start the thread attachment one eyewidth back from the eye.

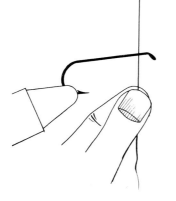

2. Wrap the thread back over itself to the point shown and trim off the excess.

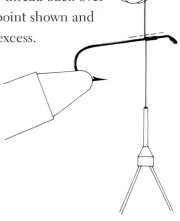

3. Pull 8 to 10 hackle fibers from a large, soft hackle feather.

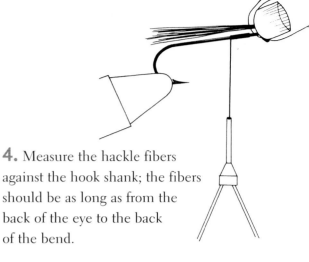

4. Measure the hackle fibers against the hook shank; the fibers should be as long as from the back of the eye to the back of the bend.

5. Holding the fibers at the measured point, move the fibers back to the start of the hook bend.

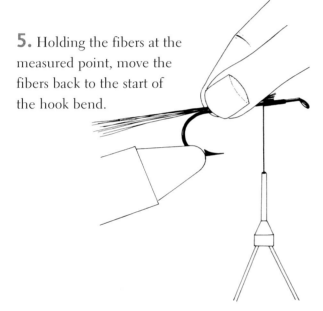

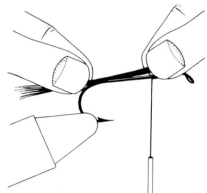

6. Grasp the hackle fibers at the bend with your left hand and move your right hand forward to the tie-in point.

7. Hold the fibers at the tie-in point with your right hand.

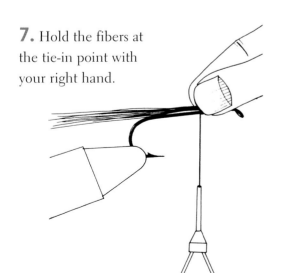

8. Grasp the fibers and the hook shank with your left hand as shown.

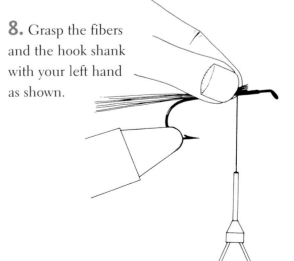

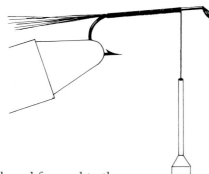

9. Tie down the butts of the fibers using the soft loop.

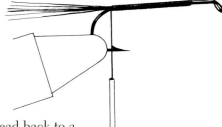

10. Wrap the thread back to a point directly opposite the barb of the hook. To keep the tail material on the top of the hook shank as you wrap, hold the fibers offset toward you as you wrap and allow the thread to carry the tail to the top as you wrap.

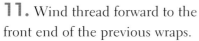

11. Wind thread forward to the front end of the previous wraps.

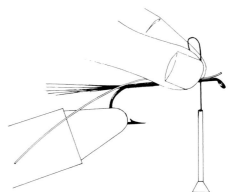

12. Attach a 4" piece of fine wire with three soft loops.

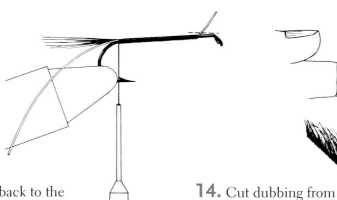

13. Bring the thread back to the point opposite the barb. Trim off the extra wire.

14. Cut dubbing from close to the skin of a piece of muskrat fur.

15. Spread dubbing fur along the thread as shown.

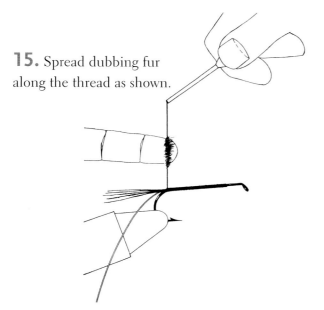

16. Grasp dubbing and thread as illustrated.

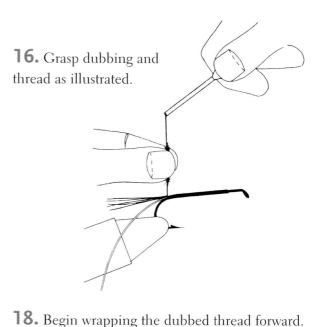

17. Spin the fur onto the thread by moving your thumb and finger in opposite directions; repeat this step (spinning in only one direction) until the fur is neatly formed into a yarn on the thread.

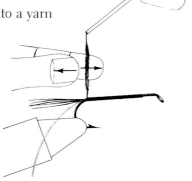

18. Begin wrapping the dubbed thread forward.

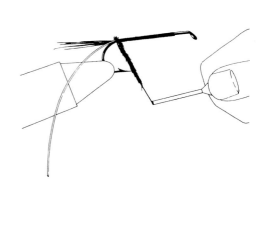

19. As you near the end of the dubbed section of thread as shown, stop wrapping and dub the next section of thread.

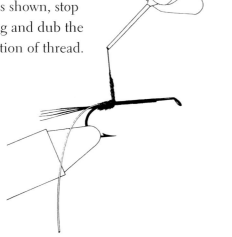

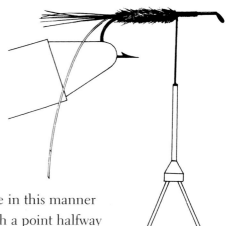

20. Continue in this manner until you reach a point halfway between the eye of the hook and the start of the bend.

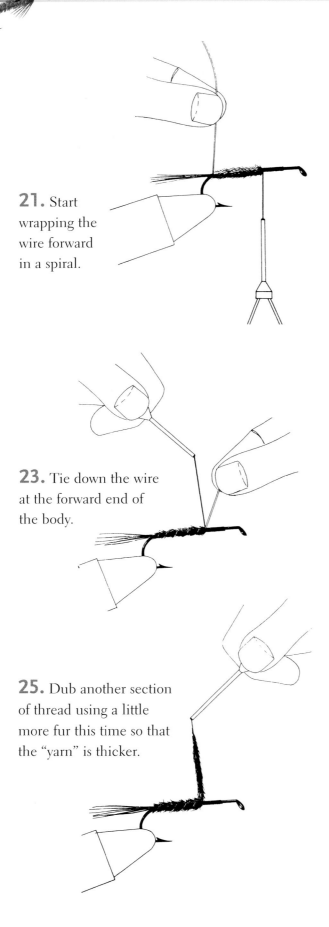

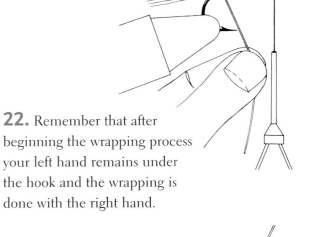

21. Start wrapping the wire forward in a spiral.

22. Remember that after beginning the wrapping process your left hand remains under the hook and the wrapping is done with the right hand.

23. Tie down the wire at the forward end of the body.

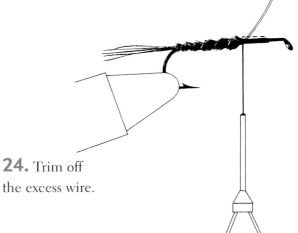

24. Trim off the excess wire.

25. Dub another section of thread using a little more fur this time so that the "yarn" is thicker.

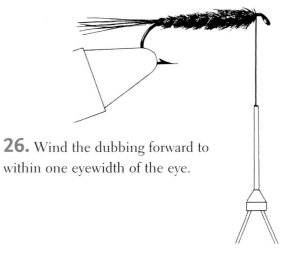

26. Wind the dubbing forward to within one eyewidth of the eye.

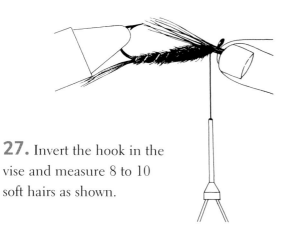

27. Invert the hook in the vise and measure 8 to 10 soft hairs as shown.

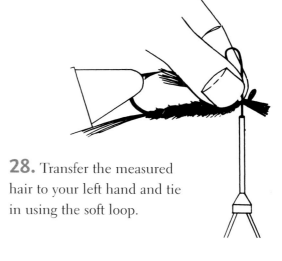

28. Transfer the measured hair to your left hand and tie in using the soft loop.

29. Cut a section from a small feather as shown and lacquer it with head cement. Position the feather section on top of the hook just behind the eye.

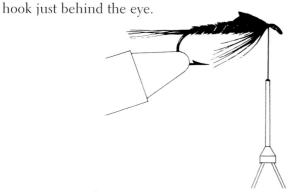

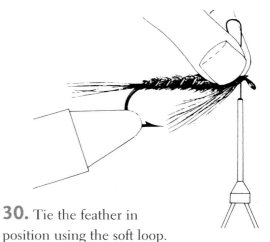

30. Tie the feather in position using the soft loop.

31 to 37. Following the steps illustrated, tie the half-hitch three times to finish the fly. For clarity, only tying off the head is shown in Steps 31 through 37; however, the other body materials are actually on the hook, as in Step 30.

31.

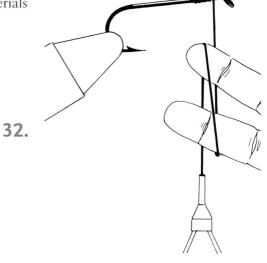

32.

33.

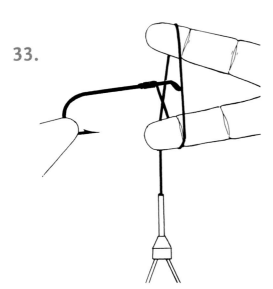

34.

35.

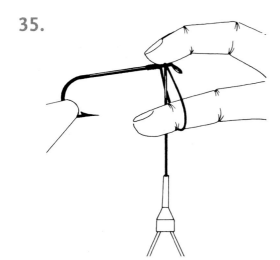

36.

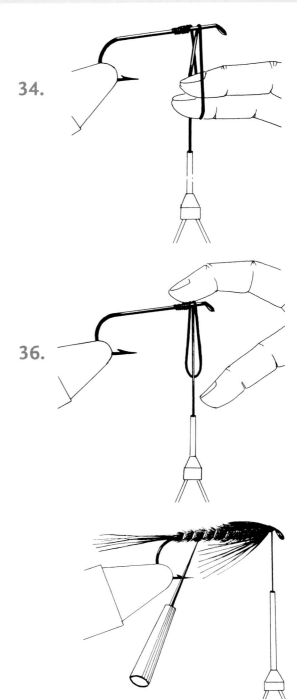

37.

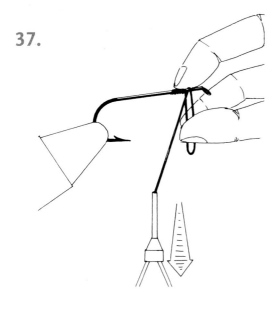

38. Pick out tufts of dubbing from between the wire wraps with a dubbing needle.

39. The finished fly.

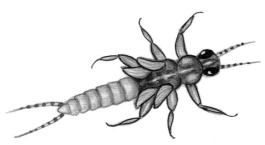

STONEFLY
NYMPH

THIS IS A VERY GOOD STONEFLY NYMPH PATTERN that Don started tying about 40 or 45 years ago; it has become a standby in many fly boxes. Its success is most likely the result of many factors: it is a realistic imitation of the insect, it is tied with enough natural materials to have the needed animation, and it sinks like a rock to get down deep in the fast water where the natural insect is found.

The tail on this pattern is made of fibers taken from the short side of a goose quill; this is a good technique to remember for the tailing of many of the short-tailed nymphs. The abdomen is a rubber band for the lighter colors, or a strip cut from a bicycle inner tube for the very dark imitations. Latex sheet material may be used by cutting rubber-band-sized strips from it. For the wing case we used a section of turkey quill, but goose quill or pheasant tail sections would be just as effective. The thorax area is heavily dubbed with a hackle wound through it to imitate legs and to provide animation.

Although this pattern involves a lot of steps, it is not difficult to tie. The only thing that is likely to give you a problem is wrapping the rubber band so that you get a nicely tapered body. The key to this step is to stretch the rubber band when you start wrapping and then decrease the tension with each wrap as you go forward. Each wrap should overlap the previous one by about one-third of the width of the rubber band.

1. Start by attaching the thread at the center of the hook shank as shown (halfway between the back of the eye and the start of the bend).

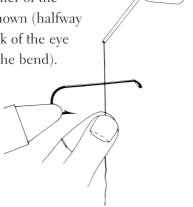

2. Wrap the thread forward four or five turns.

3. Wrap the thread back over itself and trim off the tag end.

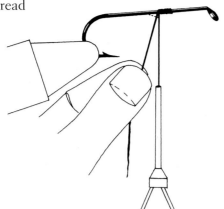

4. Wrap the thread to the start of the bend and form a lump at the rear of the wraps.

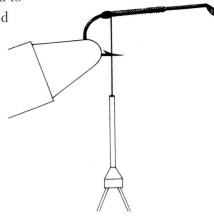

5. Cut two fibers from the leading (narrow) edge of a goose quill.

6. Trim the two fibers to equal length.

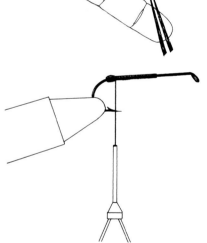

7. Tie in one of the fibers on the back side of the hook. Be certain to tighten the soft loop behind the lump.

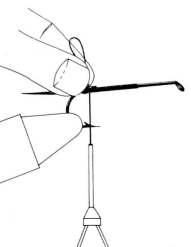

8. Tie in the second fiber on the front side of the hook in the same manner.

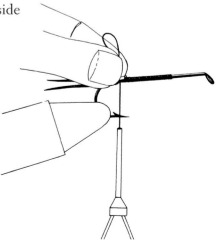

9. Wind the thread forward to the front of the wrappings.

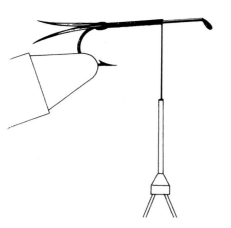

10. Trim the end of a flat rubber band at a diagonal and anchor it with at least five or six wraps of thread as shown.

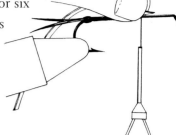

11. Stretch the rubber band to the rear and wrap the thread back to the forward end of the lump.

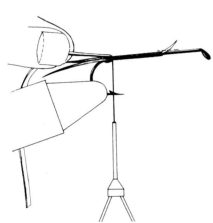

12. Wind the thread forward to the original tie-in point.

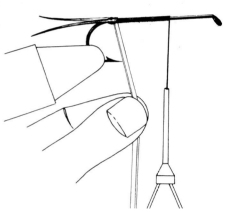

13. Begin wrapping the rubber band forward; stretch it as you wrap.

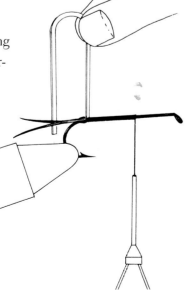

14. Maintain tension as you pass the rubber band to your left hand.

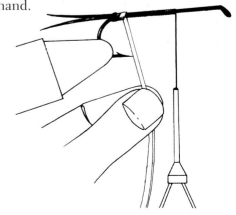

15. Continue wrapping with a slight overlap.

16. Decrease tension slightly with each wrap; as you decrease tension, the rubber band will thicken and produce a tapered body.

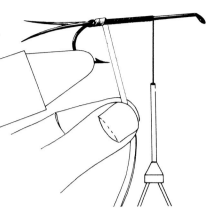

17. Maintain tension as you pass the rubber band from your left hand to your right hand.

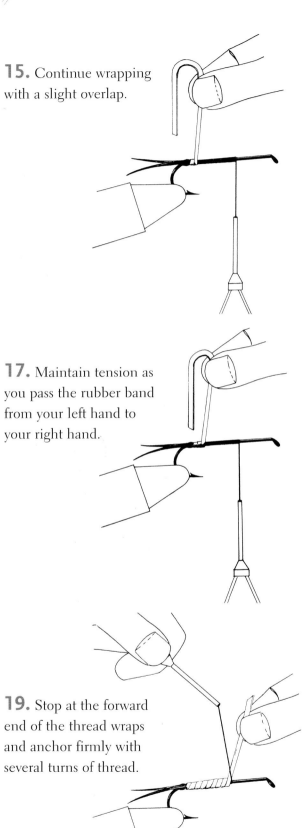

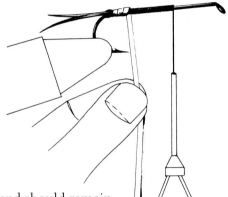

18. Your left hand should remain under the hook while your right hand does the actual wrapping.

19. Stop at the forward end of the thread wraps and anchor firmly with several turns of thread.

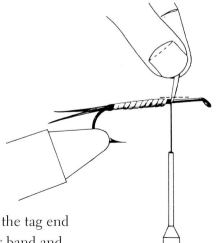

20. Stretch the tag end of the rubber band and trim off the excess.

21. Wrap the thread forward about $1/4$".

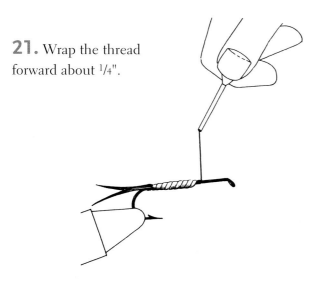

22. Cut a section of turkey quill with a width of one-third the length of the hook shank.

23. Attach the end of the quill section, using a soft loop.

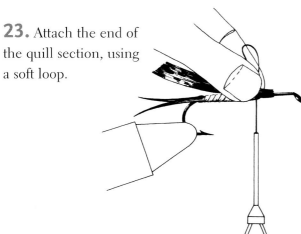

24. Select a soft hackle of the size shown.

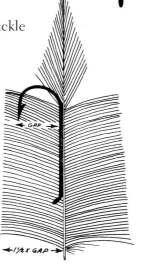

GAP

1½ x GAP

25. Cut a few flues from each side of the hackle stem and tie in by the stem butt.

26. Cut a patch of dubbing from rabbit fur, close to the skin.

27. Spread the dubbing along a section of the thread.

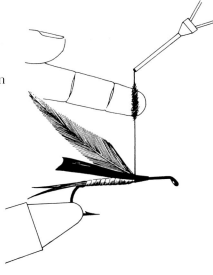

28. Hold the dubbing as shown.

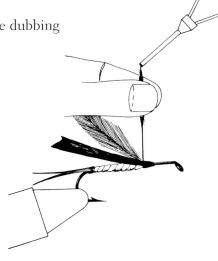

29. Spin the fur onto the thread by moving your thumb and finger in opposite directions; repeat the spinning technique until a smooth fur "yarn" is formed.

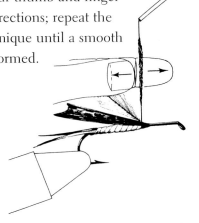

30. Slide the dubbing down the thread to the hook shank.

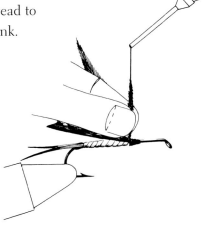

31. Begin wrapping the dubbing forward.

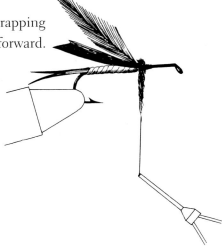

32. Stop the dubbing at a point one eyewidth back from the eye of the hook.

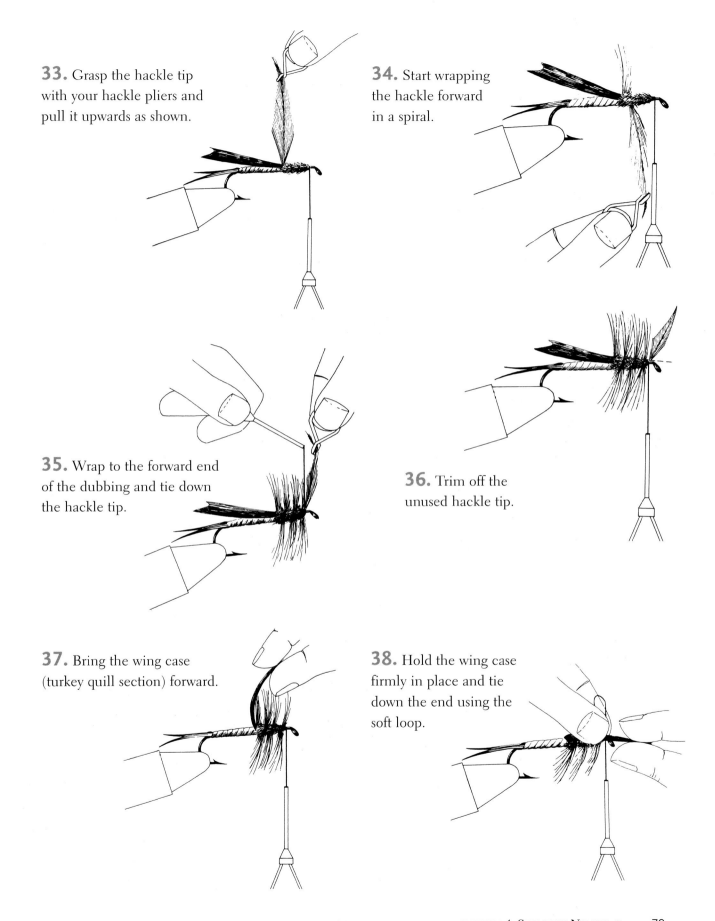

33. Grasp the hackle tip with your hackle pliers and pull it upwards as shown.

34. Start wrapping the hackle forward in a spiral.

35. Wrap to the forward end of the dubbing and tie down the hackle tip.

36. Trim off the unused hackle tip.

37. Bring the wing case (turkey quill section) forward.

38. Hold the wing case firmly in place and tie down the end using the soft loop.

39. Trim off the excess quill.

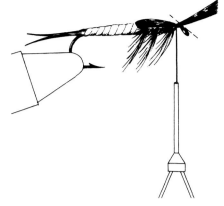

40 through 46. Tie the half-hitch three times to complete the fly. For clarity, only tying off the head is shown in Steps 40 through 46; however, the other body materials are actually on the hook, as in Step 39.

40.

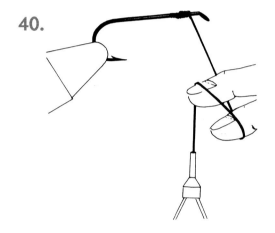

41.

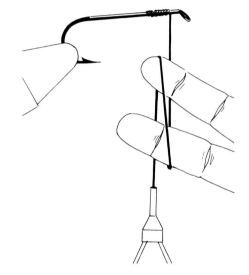

42.

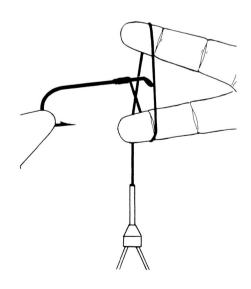

43.

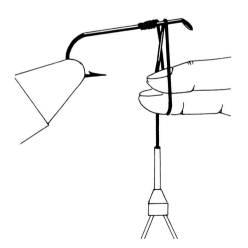

44.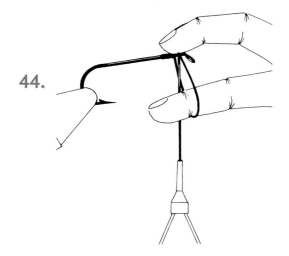

45.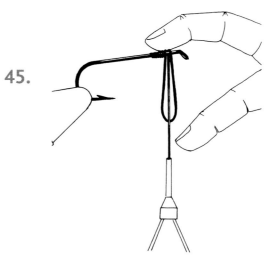

46.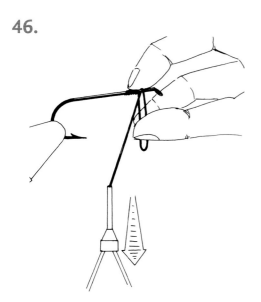

47. The finished fly.

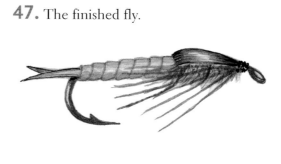

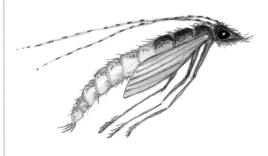

CADDISFLY

PUPA

ALTHOUGH THIS PATTERN IS NOT A HIGHLY REALISTIC IMITATION of the insect, it does offer a general appearance of the pupa, and it is very effective.

The wing case, as we illustrate it, is from a goose quill; the body is wool yarn; and the soft antennae are imitated with a hackle wound at the head. The wing case could also be made from a turkey quill section, a section of pheasant tail, or even a strip of floss. You could use dubbing for the body, but peacock would work, and so would many other materials. Instead of a wound hackle at the head, you might choose to use a throat hackle or very small hackle tips tied in on either side of the hook to represent emerging wings.

This is the first time that you will be winding hackle, so pay particular attention to the steps involved. Be especially aware of the correct proportion of the hackle; the hackle should have fibers that are 1 1/2 times the gap of the hook (see Step 16); to easily make this measurement, hold the hackle across the underside of the hook and flare the hackle as it will be when it is wrapped.

1. Start wrapping two eyewidths back from the eye. The thread should be on the near side of the hook.

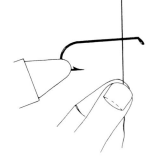

2. Wrap over the top of the hook (away from you) to a point one eyewidth back from the eye.

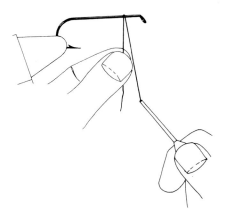

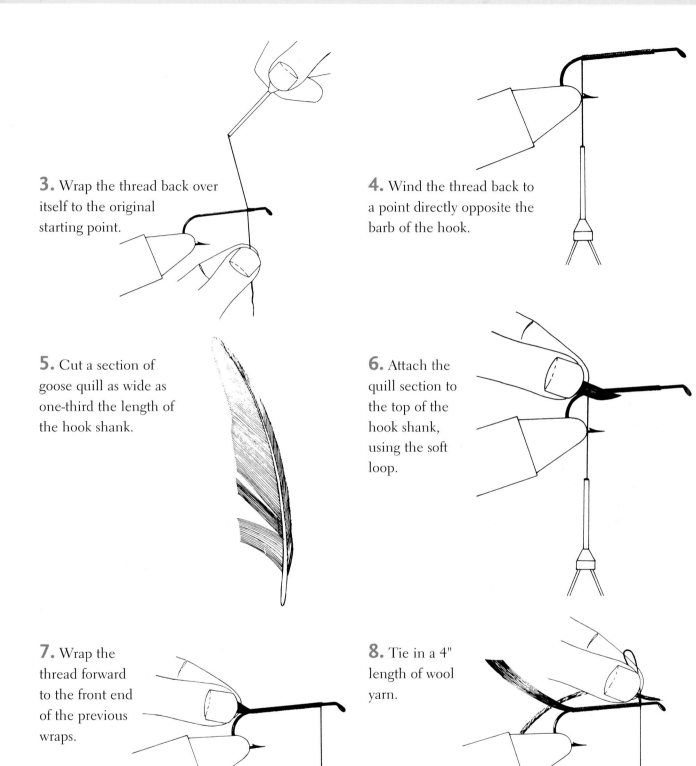

3. Wrap the thread back over itself to the original starting point.

4. Wind the thread back to a point directly opposite the barb of the hook.

5. Cut a section of goose quill as wide as one-third the length of the hook shank.

6. Attach the quill section to the top of the hook shank, using the soft loop.

7. Wrap the thread forward to the front end of the previous wraps.

8. Tie in a 4" length of wool yarn.

9. Trim off the tag end of the wool and wind the thread to the rear of the body.

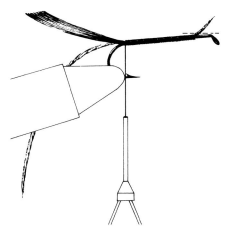

10. Bring the thread forward to the front end of the body.

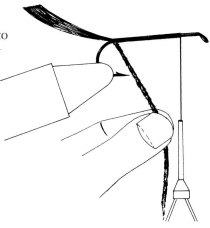

11. Wrap the wool toward the eye of the hook.

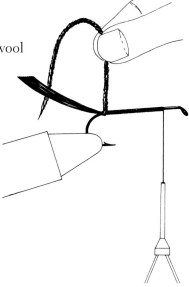

12. Stop wrapping the wool at the forward end of the body and tie it down.

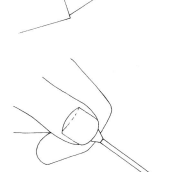

13. Trim off the excess.

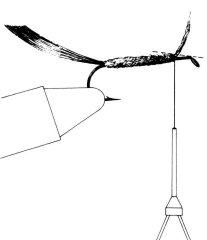

14. Pull the quill section forward as shown.

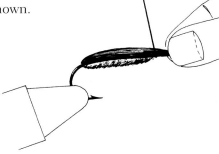

15. Tie down the end of the quill and cut off the excess.

16. Select a hackle of the proper proportion to the hook.

17. Tie the hackle in by its butt using the soft loop.

18. Begin wrapping the hackle.

19. Wind the hackle to within one eyewidth of the eye and tie it down.

20. Flare the hackle to the rear with your left hand and wrap two turns back on it; wrap forward to form the head and tie the half-hitch three times. Lacquer the head.

21. The finished fly.

MIDGE
PUPA

THIS MIDGE PUPAL IMITATION SHOULD LOOK FAMILIAR TO YOU; it is basically the same fly we tied as an imitation of the midge larva (Pattern 2). Since we want to represent the pupal stage, we have added a wing case. For the wing case we have chosen a turkey quill section but, as we mentioned in tying the stonefly nymph, pheasant or goose quill would work just as well. For the throat on this pattern, you might use soft hair or fibers from a soft feather, such as a partridge's. Just as in the larval imitation, the hook size range should be from #16 to #24, but you should practice first on a #12 or #14.

1. Start wrapping two eyewidths back from the eye. The thread should be on the near side of the hook.

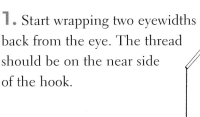
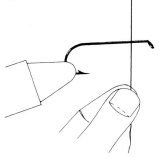

2. Wrap over the top of the hook (away from you) to a point one eyewidth back from the eye.

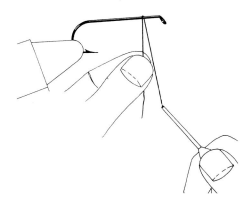

3. Wrap the thread back over itself to the original starting point.

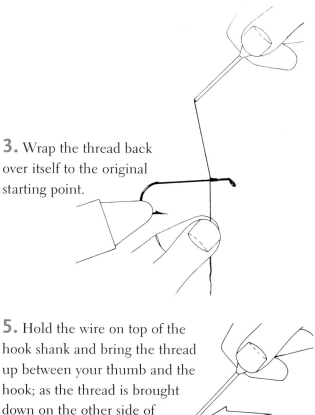

4. Hold a 4" piece of fine brass wire in your left hand as shown.

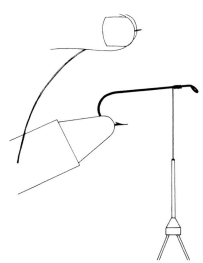

5. Hold the wire on top of the hook shank and bring the thread up between your thumb and the hook; as the thread is brought down on the other side of the hook, hold the thread in a soft loop.

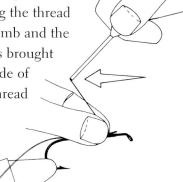

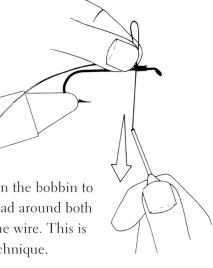

6. Pull down on the bobbin to tighten the thread around both the hook and the wire. This is the soft-loop technique.

7. Holding the wire with your left hand so that it stays on the top of the hook shank, start wrapping the thread to the rear of the hook.

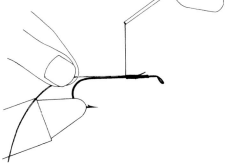

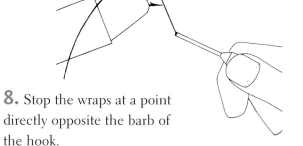

8. Stop the wraps at a point directly opposite the barb of the hook.

9. Wrap the thread forward to the original tie-in point and trim off the excess wire.

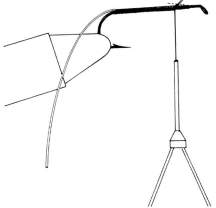

10. Hold a 5" piece of floss on the top of the hook shank with the left hand. Pinching both the floss and the hook, bring the thread up between the thumb and the hook and hold the thread in a soft loop as you bring the thread down on the back side of the hook. Pull down on the bobbin to tighten the thread around the hook and floss. Repeat three times to anchor the end of the floss.

11. Wrap the thread to a point opposite the barb of the hook; trim off the short end of the floss at the front of the hook. Wind thread forward to the original tie-in point.

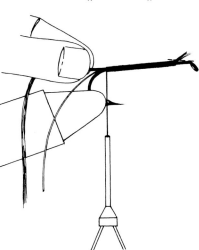

12. Start wrapping the wire forward by wrapping away from yourself with your right hand.

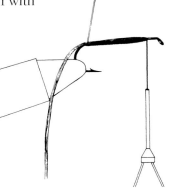

13. Pass the wire to your left hand under the hook. Your left hand stays in this position.

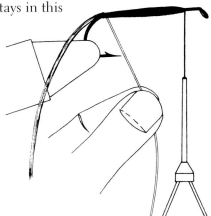

14. Pick the wire up from your left hand and begin another turn around the hook.

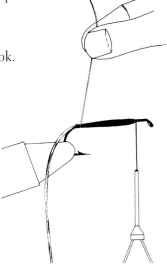

15. Pass the wire to your left hand under the hook.

16. Continue wrapping in the same manner, spiraling the wire as shown to the front of the thread wraps. Tie down the wire and trim off the excess.

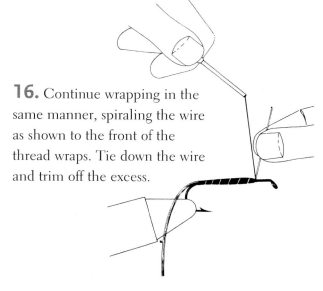

17. Begin wrapping the floss forward (away from you, over the top) with your right hand.

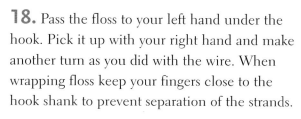

18. Pass the floss to your left hand under the hook. Pick it up with your right hand and make another turn as you did with the wire. When wrapping floss keep your fingers close to the hook shank to prevent separation of the strands.

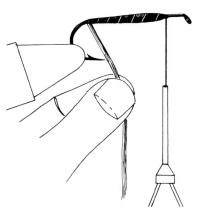

19. Wrap in this manner to the front of the thread wraps and tie the floss down.

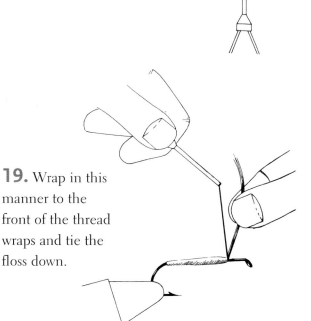

20. Trim off the excess floss.

21. Cut a section of turkey quill with a width of one-third the length of the hook shank.

22. Attach the end of the quill section, using a "soft loop."

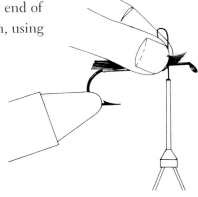

23. Trim off the tip of the quill section.

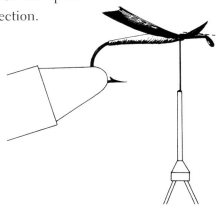

24. Cut a patch of dubbing from rabbit fur, close to the skin.

25. Spread the dubbing along a section of the thread.

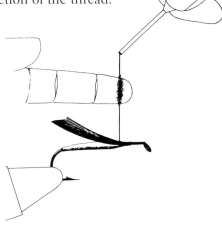

26. Hold the dubbing as shown.

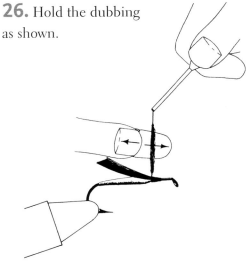

27. Spin the fur onto the thread.

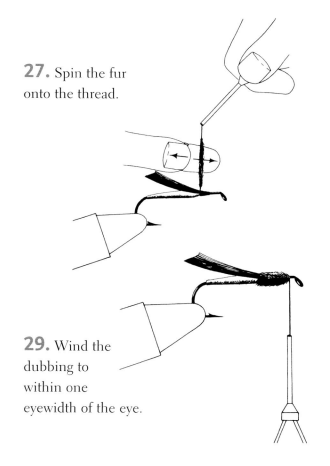

28. Start wrapping the dubbing at the forward end of the quill section.

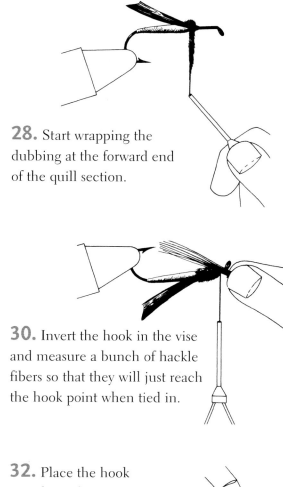

29. Wind the dubbing to within one eyewidth of the eye.

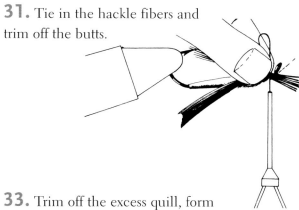

30. Invert the hook in the vise and measure a bunch of hackle fibers so that they will just reach the hook point when tied in.

31. Tie in the hackle fibers and trim off the butts.

32. Place the hook upright in the vise, bring the quill section forward, and tie it down.

33. Trim off the excess quill, form the head, and tie off with three half-hitches. Lacquer the head.

34. The finished fly.

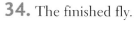

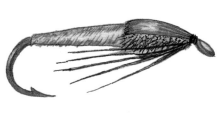

MAYFLY
EMERGER

FOR AN IMITATION OF A MAYFLY EMERGER, we have chosen a classic wet-fly pattern. You'll remember that as the mayfly nymph begins its trip to the surface to emerge, the wings may be starting to unfurl; this is displayed by the quill wing on this pattern. The tail is a bunch of soft hackle fibers, the body is peacock, the wing is made from sections of duck quill, and soft hackle is used to represent the legs and antennae.

There are many wet-fly patterns that are tied in the same basic manner. Some use floss for the body, some use dubbing. Chenille and wool are also used in some patterns.

Tying a quill wing like the one we make here is often the most difficult technique for the beginner to learn. We can't overemphasize the importance of holding the wing FIRMLY in place as you tie the soft loop to anchor it. Tighten two soft loops around the quill sections before relaxing your hold on the wings. Another common problem is the tendency to use quill sections that are too wide; each section should be about one-third as wide as the hook shank is long.

1. Start the thread attachment one eyewidth back from the eye.

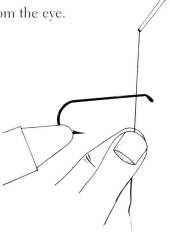

2. Wrap back on the thread to the point shown and trim off the excess.

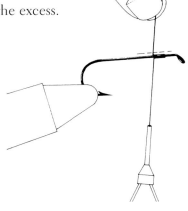

3. Pull 8 to 10 hackle fibers from a large, soft hackle feather.

4. Measure the hackle fibers against the hook shank; the fibers should be as long as from the back of the eye to the back of the hook's bend.

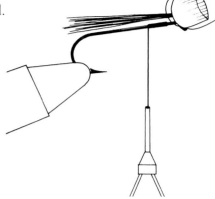

5. Holding the fibers at the measured point, move the fibers back to the start of the hook bend.

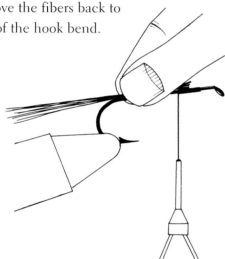

6. Grasp the hackle fibers at the bend with your left hand and move your right hand forward to the tie-in point.

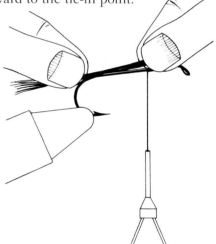

7. Hold the fibers at the tie-in point with your right hand.

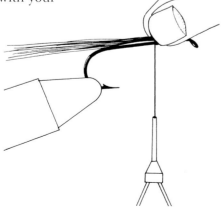

8. Grasp the fibers and the hook shank with your left hand as shown.

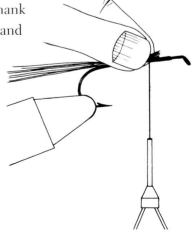

9. Tie down the butts of the fibers using the soft loop.

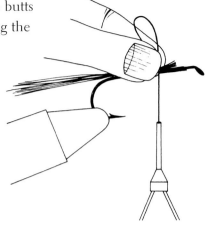

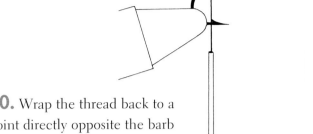

10. Wrap the thread back to a point directly opposite the barb of the hook. To keep the tail material on the top of the hook shank as you wrap, hold the fibers offset toward you as you wrap and allow the thread to carry the tail to the top as you wrap.

11. Wind thread forward to the front end of the previous wraps.

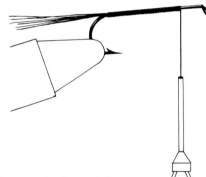

12. Hold two pieces of peacock herl on top of the shank and tie in, using the soft loop.

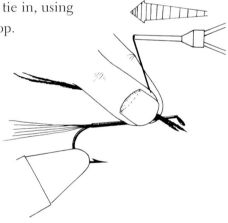

13. Remember, to tie the soft loop you must first bring the thread back between your thumb and finger to form the loop and then pull straight down with the bobbin while holding the material firmly in place.

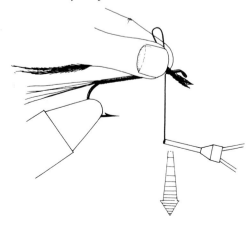

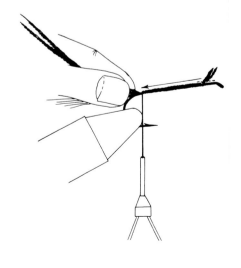

15. Wind the thread forward to the front of the previous wraps.

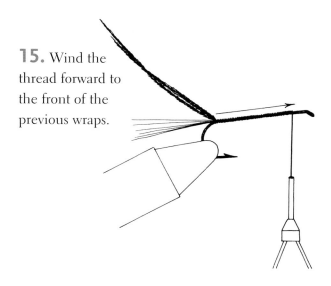

16. Start winding the herl forward with the right hand.

17. Don't forget that the left hand should remain under the hook as the right hand does the actual wrapping.

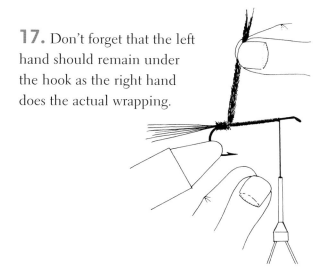

18. Wrap the herl forward to the front of the thread wraps.

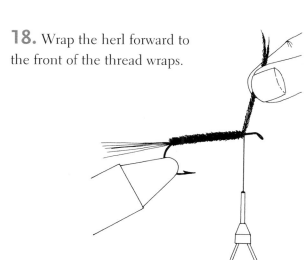

19. Hold the herl tips in your right hand and the bobbin in your left hand.

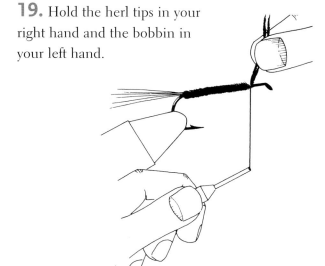

20. Pass the bobbin over the top of the hook and drop it on the back side to tie down the herl.

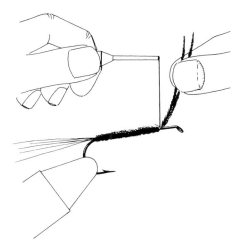

21. Trim off the herl tips.

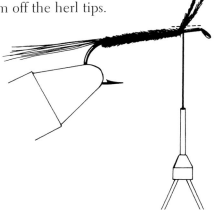

22. Wrap the thread forward to just behind the eye.

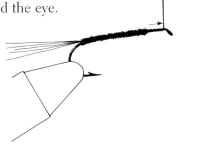

23. Wrap back to the forward end of the body.

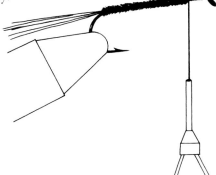

24. Select a pair of duck quills (make sure you have a right and a left, as shown).

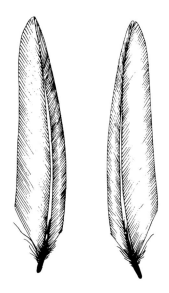

25. Split out an equal section from each quill with your bodkin and cut as shown.

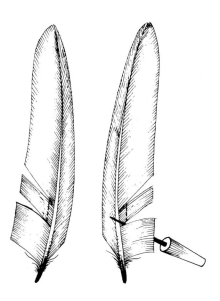

26. Notice that the sections have opposite curves. Wet the tip of your finger and lay one section on your finger with the concave side up; place the other section over it with the concave side down and align them evenly.

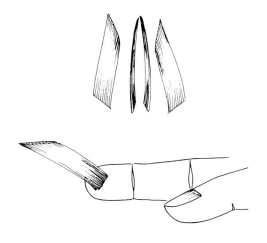

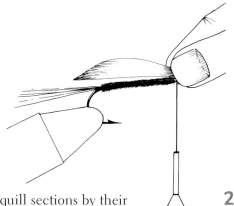

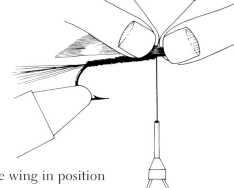

27. Holding the quill sections by their butts, measure their length against the hook shank. Their length should equal the distance from the back of the eye to the back of the bend.

28. Hold the wing in position on the hook shank and pass the sections to your left hand.

29. Notice that the finger and thumb are pinching both the quill sections and the hook.

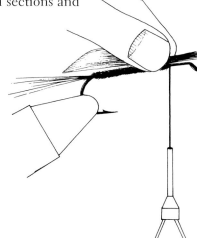

30. Form a soft loop and hold the wing firmly in position as the loop is tightened. Repeat the soft loop again before relaxing your grip on the wing.

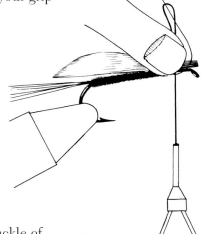

31. Wrap forward to within one eyewidth of the eye and remove the wing butts.

32. Select a hackle of the proper proportion to the hook.

33. Attach the hackle just forward of the wing and begin wrapping the hackle.

34. Wind four turns of hackle and tie down the tip.

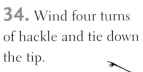

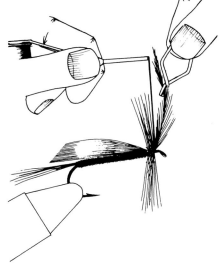

35. Trim off the hackle tip.

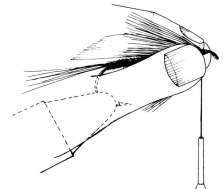

36. Sweep the hackle to the rear with your left hand and wrap back on it so that it remains in this flared position. Form the head, tie off with three half-hitches, and lacquer the head.

37. The finished fly.

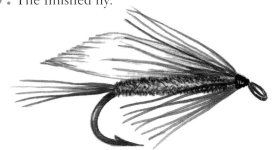

MAYFLY ADULT WITH QUILL WING

THE MAYFLY ADULT IMITATIONS ARE THE MOST USED DRY FLIES; for this reason we are going to illustrate how to tie four different types of these flies (Patterns 8 through 11). The main difference among the types is the method of wing construction.

Pattern 8 is tied using a quill wing as you did for the mayfly emerger. Watch it, though, for there are some minor changes. Here the quill sections are reversed in reference to each other; for this pattern we want the convex sides of the wings together. Also there is a variation in the tying-in step: notice that the wing is attached *before* the body is wrapped and that it is tied in the opposite direction (tip out over the eye of the hook).

1. Attach the tying thread just forward of the hook point.

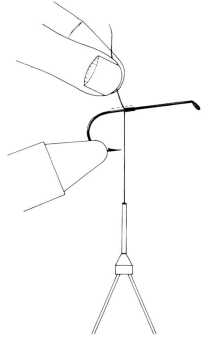

2. Pull 8 to 10 hackle fibers from a large, stiff hackle feather.

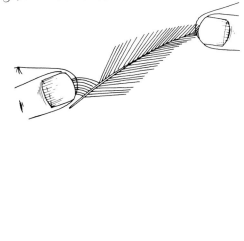

3. Measure the hackle fibers against the hook shank; the fibers should be as long as from the back of the eye to the back of the bend.

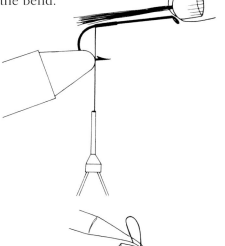

4. Holding the fibers at the measured point, move the fibers back to the start of the hook bend.

5. Tie down the tail fibers.

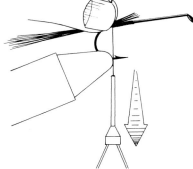

6. Trim off the fiber butts.

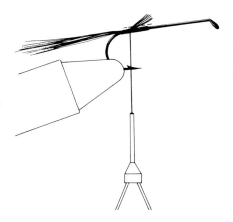

7. Select two peacock herls and tie them in as shown.

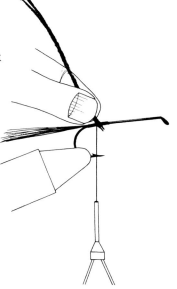

8. Wrap back on the peacock fibers to a point directly opposite the hook barb.

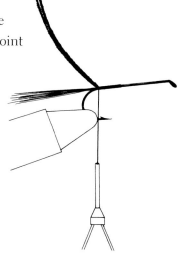

9. Wind the thread forward to a point two eyewidths back of the eye.

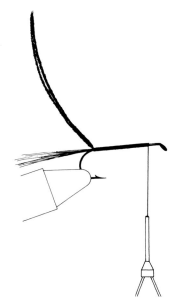

10. Select a pair of duck quills (make sure you have a right and a left, as shown).

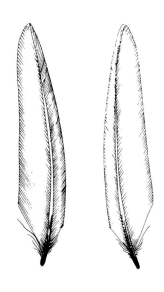

11. Split out an equal section from each quill with your bodkin and cut as shown.

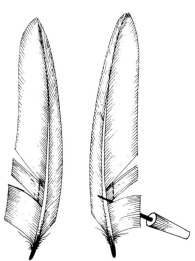

12. Notice that the sections have opposite curves. Wet the tip of your finger and lay one section on your finger with the concave side up; place the other section over it with the concave side down and align them evenly.

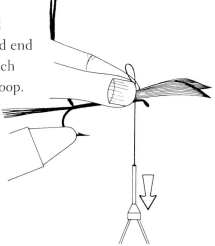

13. Holding the quill sections by their butts, measure their length against the hook shank. Length should equal the distance from the back of the bend to the back of the eye.

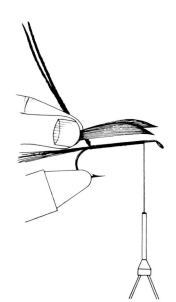

14. Move the paired sections to the forward end of the thread and attach them, using the soft loop.

15. Pull the wing erect with your left hand and wrap in front of it so that the wing will remain upright. Trim off the butt ends of the quill sections.

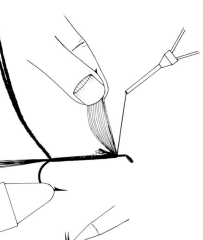

16. Wrap the thread to behind the wing.

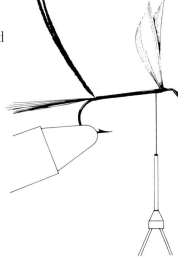

17. Begin wrapping the peacock herl forward.

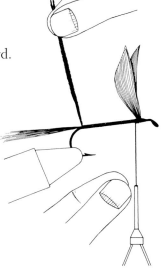

18. Wrap the herl to the rear of the wing and tie down.

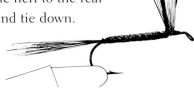

19. Trim off the herl tips.

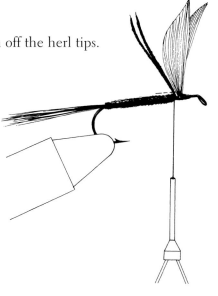

20. Select a stiff dry-fly hackle of the size shown.

21. Tie the hackle in by its butt.

22. Start wrapping the hackle behind the wing.

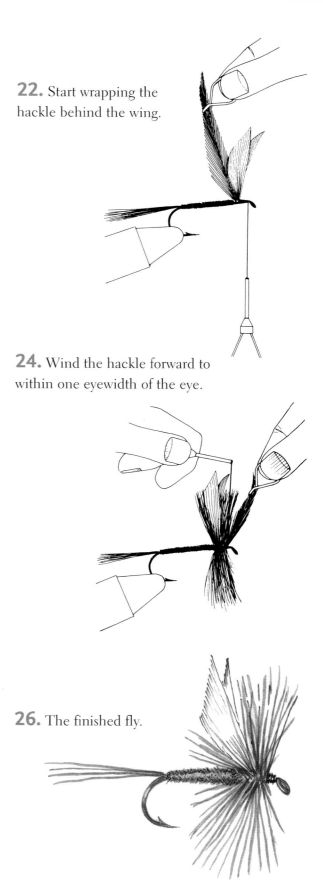

23. Make two turns behind the wing and then bring the hackle in front.

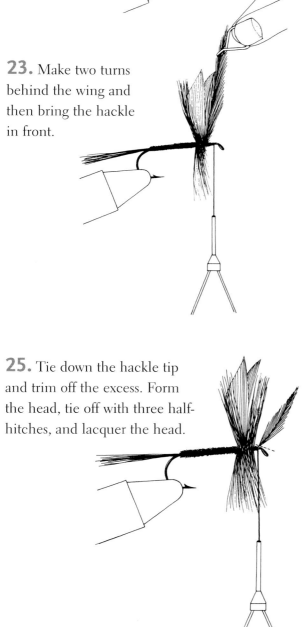

24. Wind the hackle forward to within one eyewidth of the eye.

25. Tie down the hackle tip and trim off the excess. Form the head, tie off with three half-hitches, and lacquer the head.

26. The finished fly.

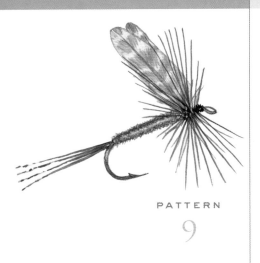

PATTERN
9

MAYFLY ADULT WITH HACKLE-TIP WING

THIS IS ANOTHER MAYFLY IMITATION, this time using a hackle-tip wing. The hackle-tip wing is easier for most people to tie than the quill wing, and it is more durable. There is one seemingly illogical point about a hackle-tip wing: the smaller the fly you are tying, the larger the hackle feather from which you select the wing. Since we need a shorter wing for the smaller flies, we have to cut it from nearer the tip of the hackle. A small hackle is so slim at the tip that a section cut from it will be too narrow for the fly. By cutting the tip from a larger hackle, it will be wider and better proportioned for use as a wing.

You should be getting the idea by now that there is nothing sacred about a particular arrangement of tail type, body material, or method of wing construction; all the individual parts may be arranged in any manner, and this is what accounts for the tremendous number of patterns that we have today. The only difference between a Mosquito and an Adams is the body: one is dubbed and the other is tied with moose mane. There are many other pairs that are identical except for the type of wing used or the method of tail construction. Tie to imitate the insects, not the patterns.

1. Begin the thread attachment midway between the point of the hook and the eye.

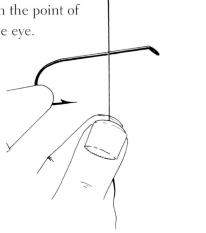

2. Wrap the thread forward to about two eyewidths back from the eye.

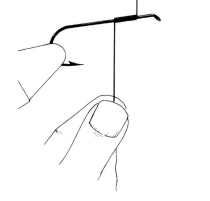

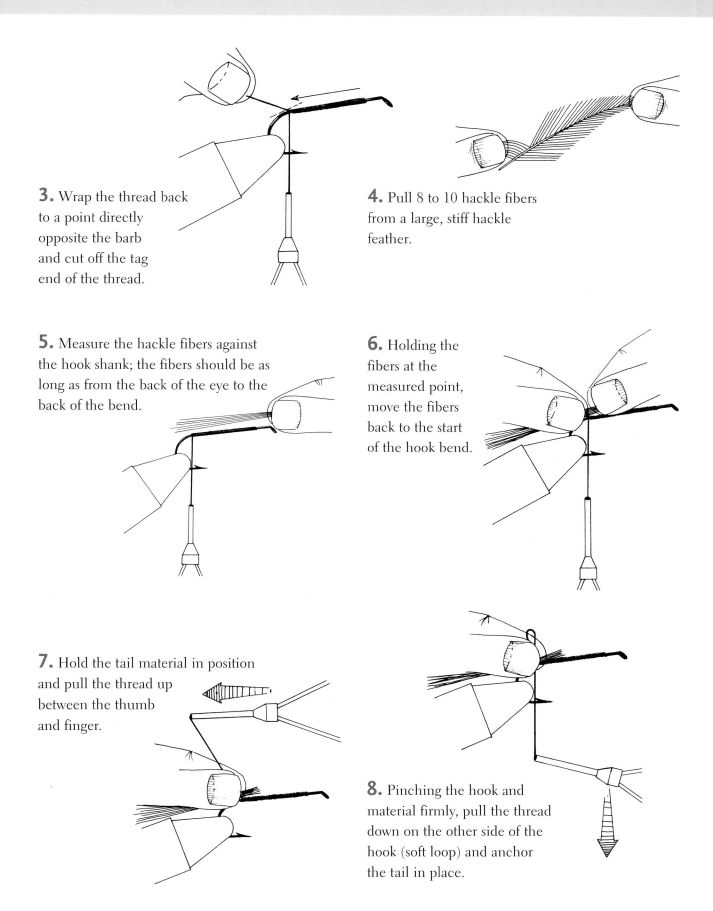

3. Wrap the thread back to a point directly opposite the barb and cut off the tag end of the thread.

4. Pull 8 to 10 hackle fibers from a large, stiff hackle feather.

5. Measure the hackle fibers against the hook shank; the fibers should be as long as from the back of the eye to the back of the bend.

6. Holding the fibers at the measured point, move the fibers back to the start of the hook bend.

7. Hold the tail material in position and pull the thread up between the thumb and finger.

8. Pinching the hook and material firmly, pull the thread down on the other side of the hook (soft loop) and anchor the tail in place.

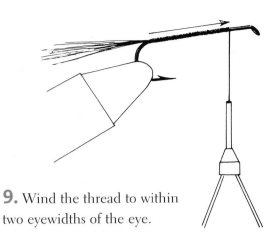

9. Wind the thread to within two eyewidths of the eye.

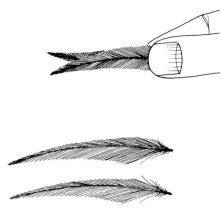

10. Select two matched hackles and place them together with the shiny sides toward each other.

11. Measure the length of the wing hackle against the hook. The wing length should be equal to the distance from the back of the eye to the back of the bend.

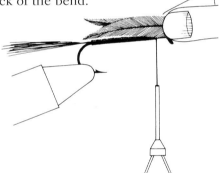

12. Hold the hackles at the measured point with your left hand; sweep the excess fibers toward the butts of the hackles; trim off the excess fibers close to the hackle stem.

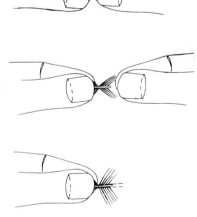

13. Tie down the hackle stems at the forward end of the thread wraps.

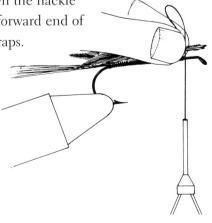

14. Pull the hackles forward and wrap behind them to hold them in the vertical position.

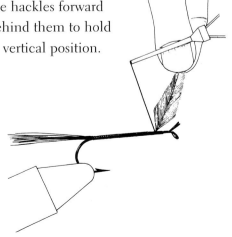

15. Trim off the hackle butts.

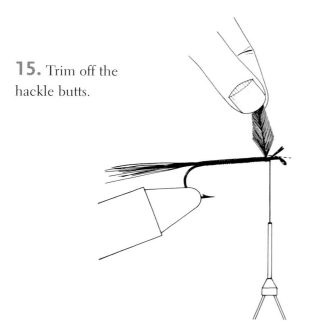

16. Wind the thread back to the rear of the thread wraps.

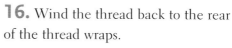
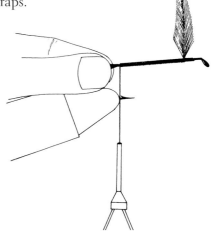

17. Spread the dubbing along the thread.

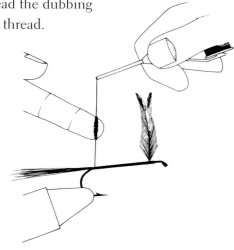

18. Spin the dubbing onto the thread.

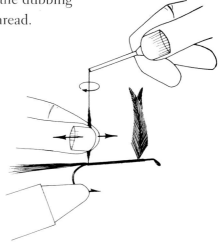

19. Start forming the dubbed body by wrapping the dubbed thread forward. Add more dubbing to thread as needed.

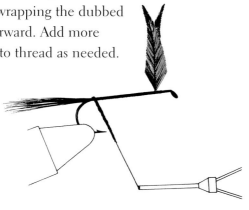

20. Bring the body forward to a point just short of the wing.

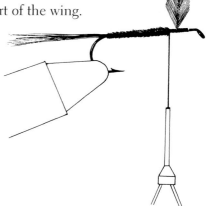

21. Tie in a hackle of the proper size behind the wing.

22. Pull the wings gently forward and start winding the hackle behind them.

23. Make two turns of hackle behind the wings.

24. Gently pull the wings upright and pass the hackle in front of the wing.

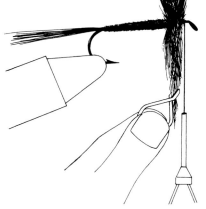

25. Wind the hackle to within one eyewidth of the eye; tie down the tip.

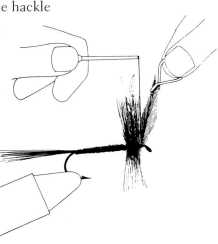

26. Trim off the hackle tip; shape the head and tie off with three half-hitches.

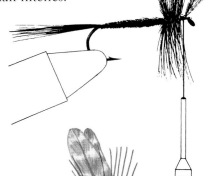

27. The finished fly.

PATTERN

10

MAYFLY ADULT WITH ROLLED WING

PATTERN 10 IS ANOTHER TYPE OF MAYFLY ADULT PATTERN. The wing construction you will be using for this fly is called a rolled wing. There are several techniques that may be employed to tie this type of wing. We are using the method that we have found easiest for most beginners to learn.

By now you should realize that proper proportion is critical in order for the finished fly to look right, particularly a dry fly. You will find that as the size of the fly decreases, this becomes even more true. The tail should be as long as the distance from the back of the eye to the back of the bend. The size of the hackle feather needs to be 1½ times the size of the gap of the hook, and the wing should be twice the size of the gap of the hook (see Figure on page 50).

The body in this pattern is made of tying thread, which is then wrapped with a stripped peacock herl to provide segmentation; therefore, you must take care as you wrap your thread to make a smooth body. The rolled wing provides a very good wing silhouette. Because it is more durable than the quill wing or the hackle-tip wing, we use it more than either of those types.

1. Attach the tying thread just forward of the hook point.

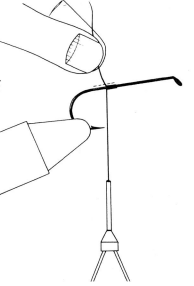

2. Pull 8 to 10 hackle fibers from a large, stiff hackle feather.

3. Measure the hackle fibers against the hook shank; the fibers should be as long as the distance from the back of the eye to the back of the bend.

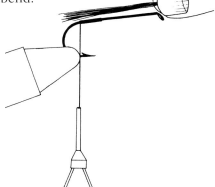

4. Holding the fibers at the measured point, move the fibers back so their butts are over the start of the hook bend.

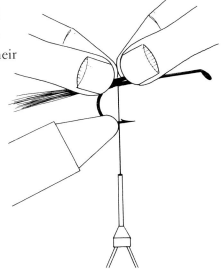

5. Tie down the tail fibers.

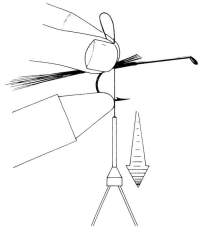

6. Trim off the fiber butts.

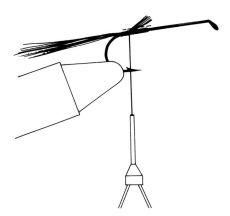

7. Cut a mallard feather as shown.

8. Wind the thread forward to about two eyewidths back from the eye. Using the center portion of the mallard feather that you just trimmed, measure for the proper wing length.

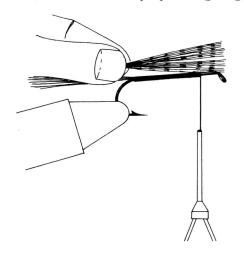

9. Hold the wing in your left hand and position the wing at the forward end of the body.

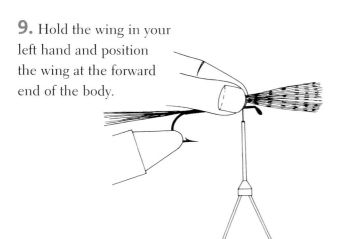

10. Tie down the wing and trim off the butt.

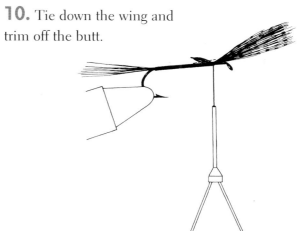

11. Gently pull the wing upright and wrap in front of it so that it will remain in position.

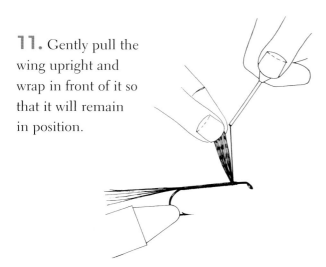

12. Select a herl from the eye of a peacock feather, and strip off the fuzz using a pencil eraser.

13. Tie in the stripped herl just behind the wing.

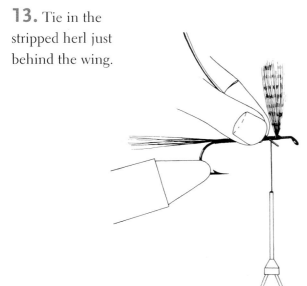

14. Wrap the thread back to a point just opposite the barb. Remember to keep the thread wrap very smooth, because it will form the body.

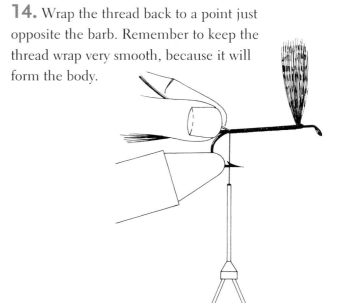

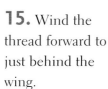

15. Wind the thread forward to just behind the wing.

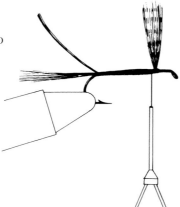

16. Gently pull the herl upright and start the wrap.

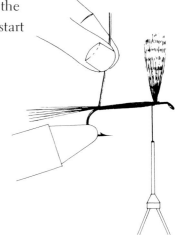

17. Wrap the herl forward in a spiral around the hook shank.

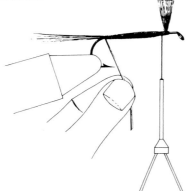

18. Tie the herl down behind the wing and trim off the excess.

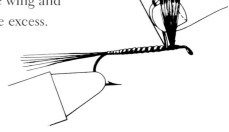

19. Tie in a hackle of the proper size (1$\frac{1}{2}$ times the gap of the hook).

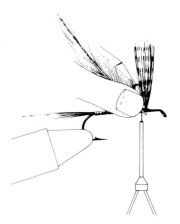

20. Start wrapping the hackle behind the wing.

21. Make two turns behind the wing.

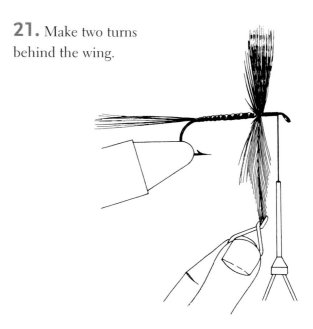

22. Bring the hackle in front of the wing and wind to within one eyewidth of the eye. Tie down the hackle tip, trim off the tip, form the head, and tie off.

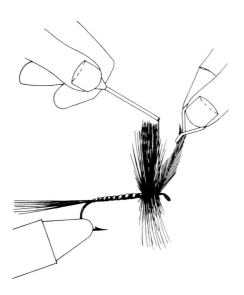

23. The finished fly.

MAYFLY IMAGO (SPINNER) STAGE

THIS PATTERN IS MEANT TO IMITATE THE IMAGO OR SPINNER STAGE of the mayfly adult. You'll remember from our discussion of mayflies that they are unique in that they undergo an additional molt after becoming adults; this is the stage at which mating takes place. After mating has occurred, many of the insects fall to the water in the spent-wing position. For this imitation, we have used hackle-tip wings, but a hair wing or hackle fibers could be (and often are) used. The body should be dressed a little slimmer than it is on the emerging adult, and the colors should be somewhat brighter than they are for the newly emerged adult patterns.

1. Attach the thread two eyewidths back from the eye and wrap to the rear of the shank. Spin a small amount of dubbing on the thread.

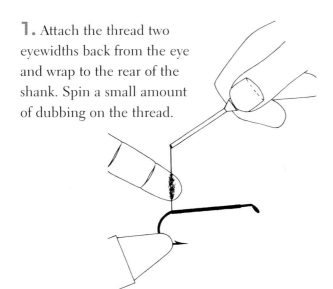

2. Wind the dubbing to produce a lump as shown. Select two stiff hairs, such as javelina or moose mane.

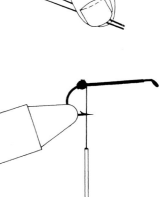

3. Tie in one hair on the back side of the hook.

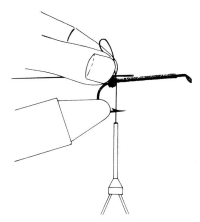

4. Tie in the second hair on the near side of the hook. Hairs should be positioned on the sides of the hook so that the dubbed lump will force them apart to form a wide V shape.

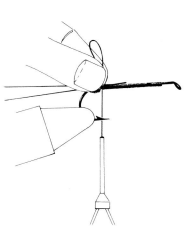

5. Dub a section of thread.

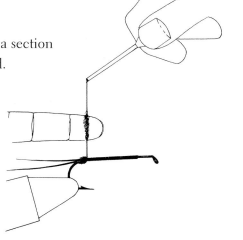

6. Form the dubbed body by winding to the position shown. You will have to apply dubbing to two or three sections of thread to form the body.

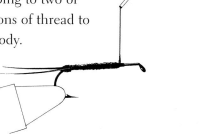

7. Measure two hackle tips for the wings.

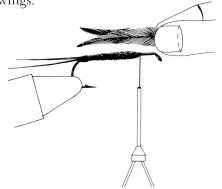

8. Pass the measured wing to your left hand.

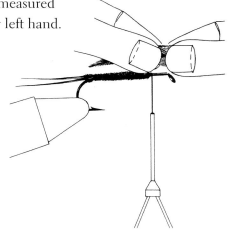

9. Trim the fibers from the hackle butts as shown.

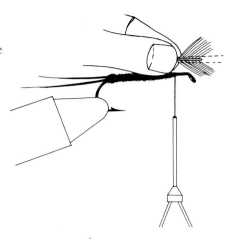

10. Tie in the hackle-tip wing at the forward end of the body.

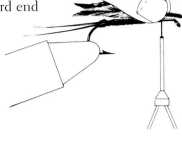

11. Gently pull the wing upright and wind behind it to hold it upright.

12. Trim off the hackle stems.

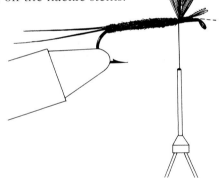

13. Pull each wing down to the horizontal position and wrap the thread from behind the near wing, across the shank, and in front of the far wing.

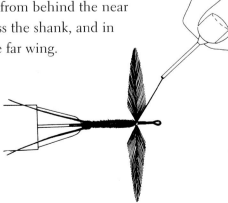

14. Bring the thread under the hook shank and up in front of the near wing.

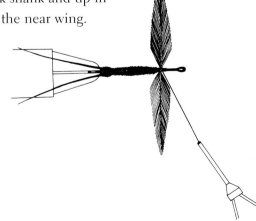

15. Take the thread diagonally across the hook shank to behind the far wing. Repeat this figure-eight wrap twice to anchor the wings in position.

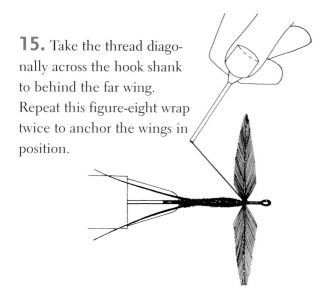

16. Gently pull the wings slightly forward and tie in a proper sized hackle.

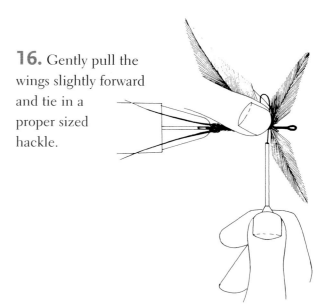

17. Start wrapping the hackle behind the wing.

18. Pull the wings back to their original position and wrap the hackle forward. Tie down the hackle tip, trim it, and finish the head of the fly.

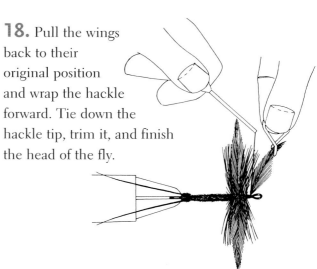

19. The finished fly.

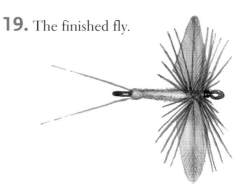

STONEFLY
ADULT

BECAUSE THE STONEFLY ADULT CARRIES ITS WINGS in a flat position over its back, it lends itself well to imitation with a hair wing. This is the most durable of the wing types and provides for very good flotation, as the fly rests on the wing in the water's surface film.

We illustrate this pattern with a split tail of two stiff hairs such as javelina or moose mane, a floss body, a squirrel-tail wing, and a double hackle. The winging method and the double hackle are the only new procedures for you to learn as you tie this imitation.

To even the ends of the squirrel-tail hairs, follow the illustrations closely. The soft loop must be used at least three times to firmly anchor the hair in place before continuing the wrapping. It is a good idea to put a drop of head cement on the hair butts of the wings after they are tied in.

You could substitute a bunch of hackle fibers or hair for the javelina or moose-hair tail. A dubbed body would provide better flotation than the floss, and there are many other hairs that would work for the wing—badger, for instance. Since the stonefly is a long-bodied insect, this imitation should be tied on a 2X or 3X long-shank hook. We use these in sizes from #4 to #14, and they are deadly when cast up into a fast run and allowed to sweep down into the head of a pool.

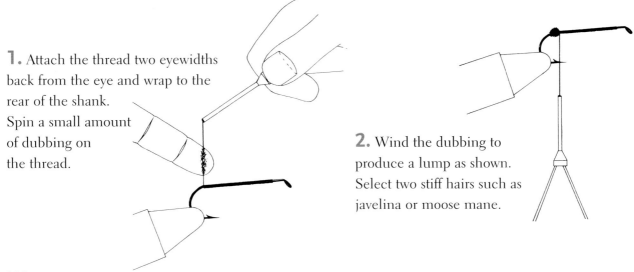

1. Attach the thread two eyewidths back from the eye and wrap to the rear of the shank. Spin a small amount of dubbing on the thread.

2. Wind the dubbing to produce a lump as shown. Select two stiff hairs such as javelina or moose mane.

3. Tie in one hair on the back side of the hook.

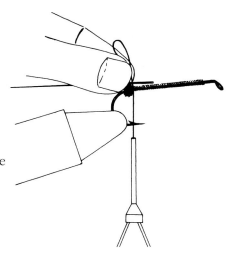

4. Tie in the second hair on the near side of the hook.
Hairs should be positioned on the sides of the hook so that the dubbed lump will force them apart to form a wide V shape.

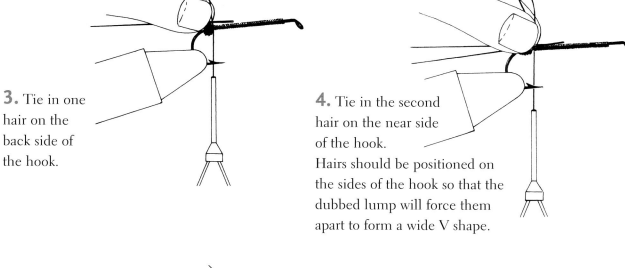

5. Advance the thread to a point two eyewidths back of the eye and tie in a piece of floss.

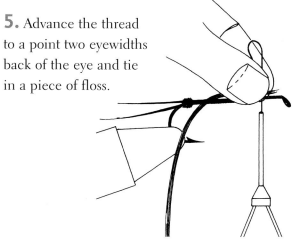

6. Wrap the thread back to the forward end of the lump.

7. Wind the thread forward to the tie-in point and trim off the excess floss.

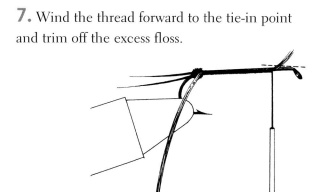

8. Wrap the floss to the forward end of the thread wrap.

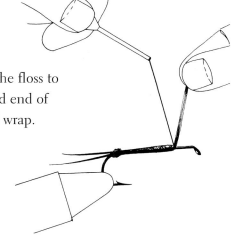

9. Tie down the floss and trim off the excess.

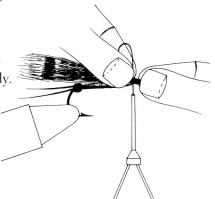

10. Cut a section of squirrel tail hair. Hold the hair by the tips in your left hand and pull out the short hairs with your right hand.

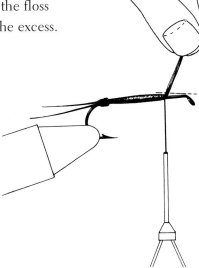

11. Tie in the hair so that it extends to the rear of the tail. Anchor it firmly.

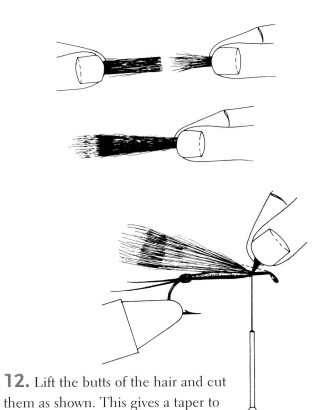

12. Lift the butts of the hair and cut them as shown. This gives a taper to the butts so that there will be less of a lump in front of the wing.

13. Select two hackles of the proper size and place them back to back.

14. Tie in the two hackles just ahead of the wing.

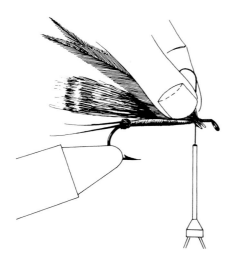

15. Grasp the rear hackle with your hackle pliers.

16. Wrap the hackle to within one eyewidth of the eye and tie it down.

17. Wrap the second hackle forward to the same point and tie it down. Trim off the hackle tips, form the head, and tie off the fly.

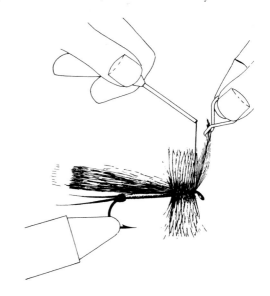

18. The finished fly.

PATTERN
13

CADDISFLY

ADULT

THE CADDISFLY ADULT IMITATION SHOWN HERE has become one of the most popular adult caddisfly imitations in Colorado. We chose it because it is a good producer and because it will require you to use many of the procedures that we have covered up to this point. The pattern can be used for hook sizes #10 to #20, and since the adult caddisfly has a long body, you should use a 2X long shank hook.

The original pattern used elk hair for the wing as we show here, but fine deer hair, caribou, or antelope could be substituted. The body is of wool yarn, although dubbing would work just as well. Notice that the palmered hackle is proportioned as if it were used at the head of the fly, 1½ times the size of the gap of the hook. The wing should extend from just behind the eye to a point halfway between the bend of the hook and the end of the tail.

1. Attach the thread two eye-widths back from the eye and wrap to the rear of the shank. Spin a small amount of dubbing on the thread.

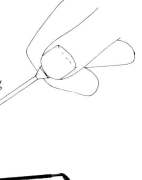

2. Wind the dubbing to produce a lump as shown. Select two stiff hairs such as javelina hairs or moose mane.

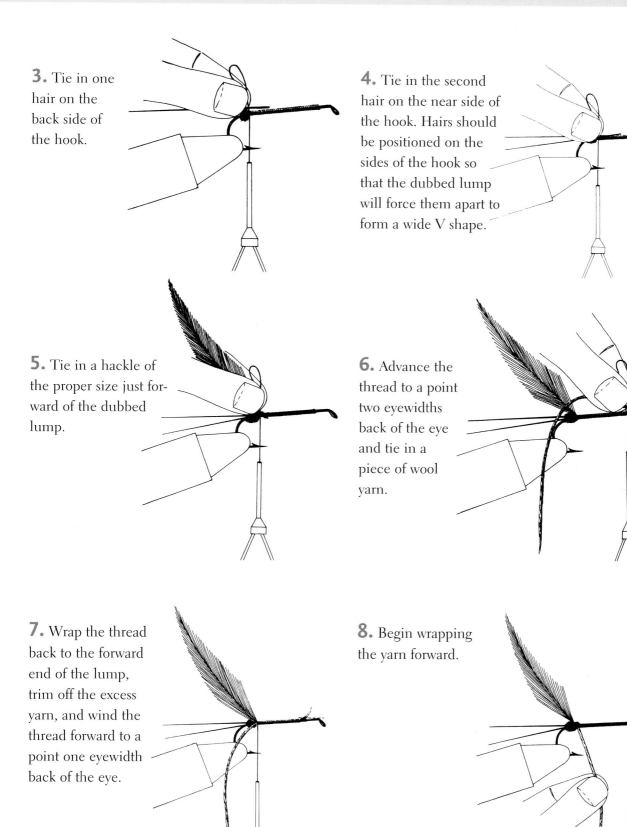

3. Tie in one hair on the back side of the hook.

4. Tie in the second hair on the near side of the hook. Hairs should be positioned on the sides of the hook so that the dubbed lump will force them apart to form a wide V shape.

5. Tie in a hackle of the proper size just forward of the dubbed lump.

6. Advance the thread to a point two eyewidths back of the eye and tie in a piece of wool yarn.

7. Wrap the thread back to the forward end of the lump, trim off the excess yarn, and wind the thread forward to a point one eyewidth back of the eye.

8. Begin wrapping the yarn forward.

9. Wrap the yarn to within one eyewidth of the eye and tie it down.

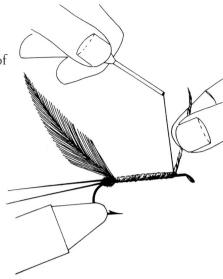

10. Trim off the excess yarn.

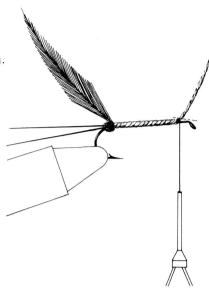

11. Palmer the hackle forward and tie it down. Trim off the hackle tip.

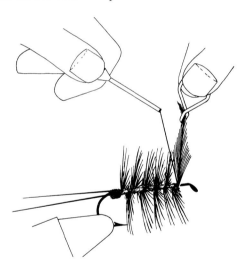

12. Cut out a small patch of elk hair, hold the tips in your left hand and pull out and discard the short hairs and underhair with your right hand.

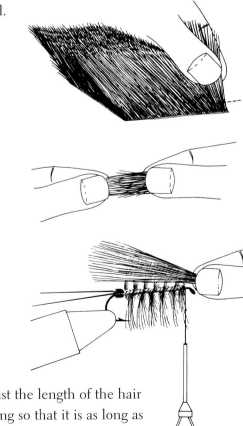

13. Adjust the length of the hair for the wing so that it is as long as from the front of the eye to the back of the bend.

14. Transfer the measured hair to your left hand and tie it down.

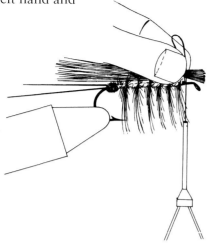

15. Trim off the hair butts at an angle as shown.

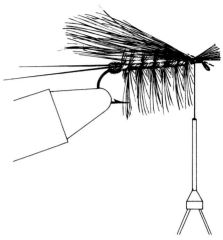

16. Shape the head with thread and tie off the fly.

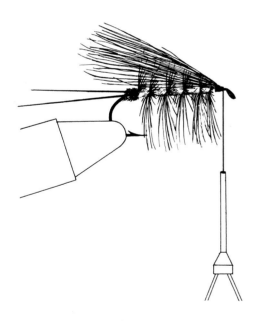

17. The finished fly.

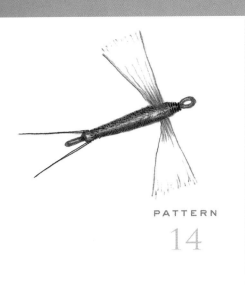

MIDGE

ADULT

THE ADULT MIDGE CARRIES ITS WINGS either in a spent position or in a flat V. We are tying a spent-wing type using polypropylene yarn for the winging material. Hackle tips can be used in the same fashion as we did on the spent-wing mayfly (Pattern 11). Hackle can be wound and then trimmed top and bottom to leave only the wing shape, or the wing can be fabricated from a bunch of hair tied in on either side of the thorax.

For a true-to-size imitation, the fly should be dressed on hooks ranging from about #18 to #24 or even smaller, and since the insect has a long, delicate abdomen, a 1X long hook could be used. Midges are found in nearly all colors from white to black, but the whites, greens, and browns are the most common.

1. Attach the thread two eyewidths back from the eye and wrap to the rear of the shank. Spin a small amount of dubbing on the thread.

2. Wind the dubbing to produce a lump as shown. Select two stiff hairs such as javelina hair or moose mane.

3. Tie in one hair on the back side of the hook.

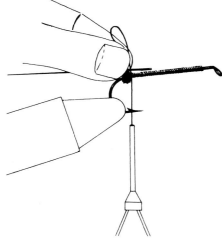

4. Tie in the second hair on the near side of the hook. Hairs should be positioned on the sides of the hook so that the dubbed lump will force them apart to form a wide V shape.

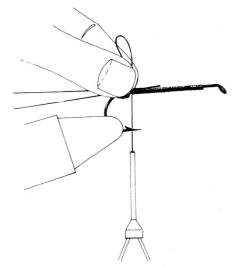

5. Dub a section of thread.

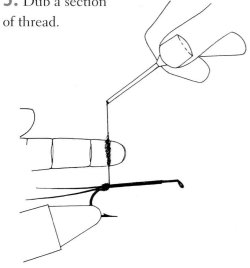

6. Form the dubbed body by winding to the position shown. You will probably need to apply dubbing to two or three sections of thread to form the body.

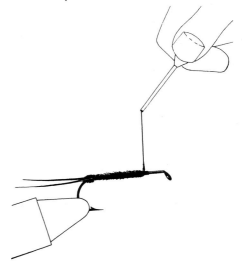

7. Measure a piece of polypropylene yarn as long as the shank of the hook plus one-half of the tail.

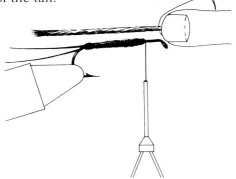

8. Cut the yarn at the measured point and pass it to your left hand.

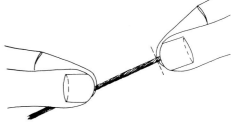

9. Tie the midpoint of the yarn down at the forward end of the body.

10. Pull the rear piece of yarn forward.

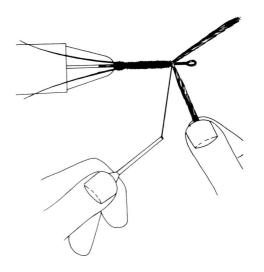

11. Wrap behind the yarn to hold it in place.

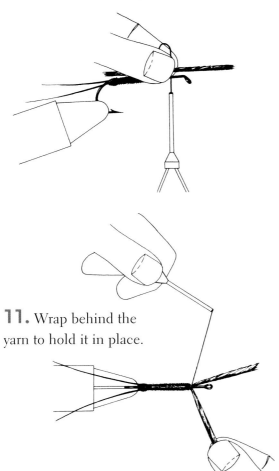

12. Pull the other piece of yarn to the rear and pass the thread in front of it to hold it in position.

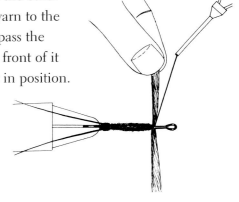

13. Figure-eight across the wing junction to anchor the wing in position.

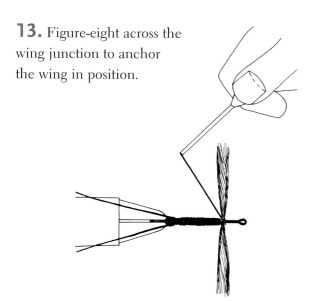

14. Dub a section of thread.

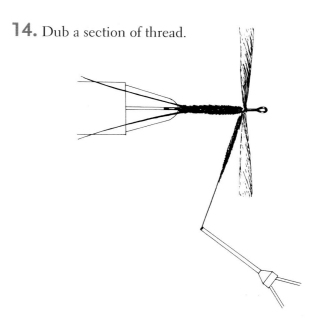

15. Figure-eight the dubbing between the wings and to within one eyewidth of the eye. Form the head and tie off the fly. Use your dubbing needle to separate the strands of yarn to form the wing shape.

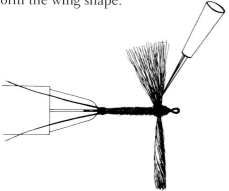

16. The finished fly.

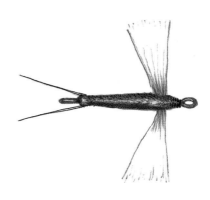

HAIR-WING
STREAMER

PATTERN 15 IS THE FIRST OF FOUR STREAMER PATTERNS we offer for you to tie. It is a hair-wing streamer, or bucktail, and is meant to imitate a small baitfish. The colors used for the wing are variable, depending on the coloration of the minnow being imitated, but the top bunch of hair should always be darker than the bottom bunch to match the dark dorsal area found on all stream fish.

In Pattern 15, we are going to have you start tying the whip finish to tie off the head of the fly. This knot is much superior to the half-hitches that you have been using. If you follow the instructions closely for the first couple of times, you shouldn't have too much trouble. There are many different ways of tying the whip finish, but we have found this method the easiest to learn.

As you wrap the tinsel body on this fly, keep the edges of the tinsel as close together as possible without overlapping. The reason for wrapping the body with tinsel in both directions is that there will be tinsel showing through any spaces between the final wraps.

1. Attach the tying thread one eyewidth back from the eye.

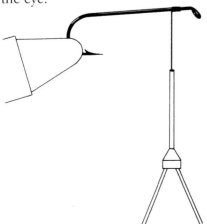

2. Tie in a 6" piece of wide flat tinsel.

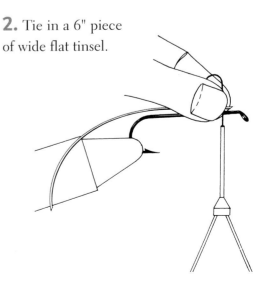

3. Trim off the tag end of the tinsel and begin wrapping the tinsel to the rear.

4. When you reach a point directly opposite the barb of the hook, reverse the wrap and start wrapping the tinsel forward.

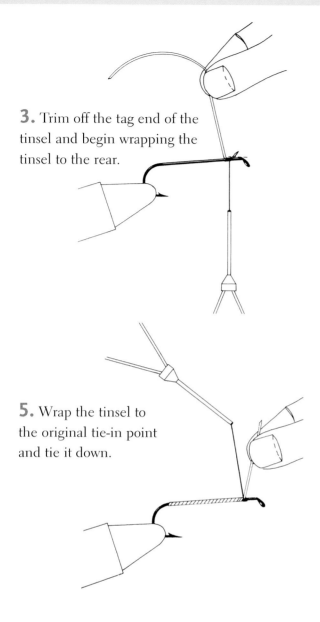

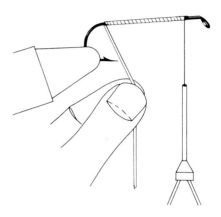

5. Wrap the tinsel to the original tie-in point and tie it down.

6. Trim off the extra tinsel.

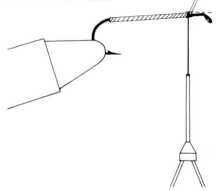

7. Invert the hook in the vise and measure a bunch of bucktail for the throat.

8. Tie in the throat.

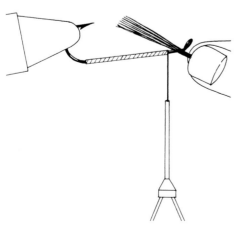

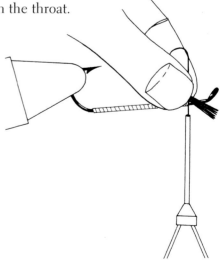

9. Measure a small bunch of light-colored bucktail for the wing and pass it to your left hand.

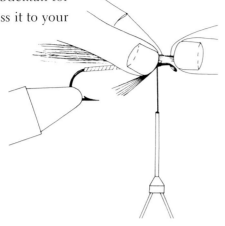

10. Tie in the wing.

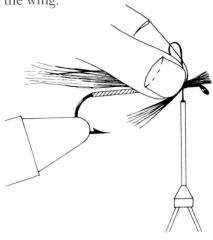

11. Trim off the butts of the hair at an angle as shown.

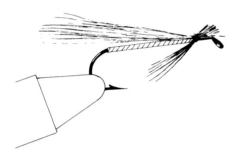

12. Wrap over the butts of the hair.

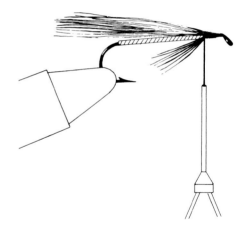

13. Measure a small bunch of darker bucktail and tie in on top of the first bunch.

14. Form a neat head with your tying thread.

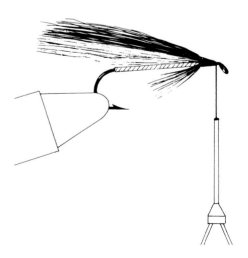

15. Lay the first two fingers of your right hand across the thread (fingernails toward you) and wrap the thread around them as shown.

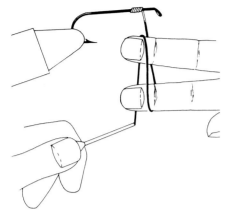

16. Rotate your hand so that your fingers are pointing up (fingernails still towards you).

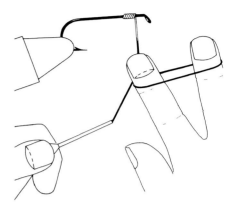

17. Raise the bobbin as you drop your middle finger.

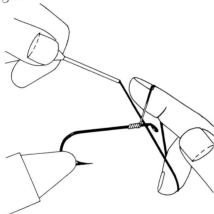

18. Pull the slack from the loop you have formed by lowering your right hand. Grasp the rear thread with your left thumb and finger and pull downward.

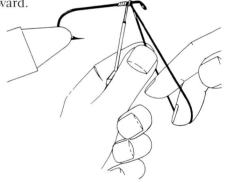

19. Take the thread from your left fingers with your right hand as shown.

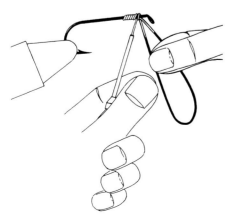

20. Wrap the thread over the hook shank and the slack section of the thread.

21. Pass the thread back to your left hand. Repeat this wrapping at least three times.

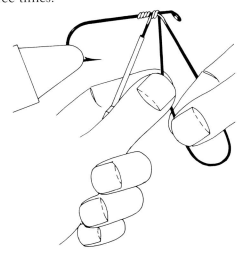

22. Pull down on the bobbin to tighten the loops around the shank and the thread. Lacquer the head.

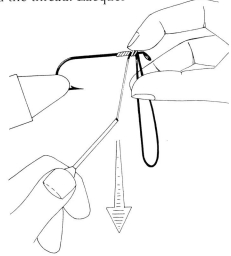

23. When the head lacquer is nearly dry, apply a drop of white lacquer to each side of the head, using the large end of a small finishing nail, to represent eyes. When the white lacquer is nearly dry, add a small dot of black lacquer, using the small end of the nail.

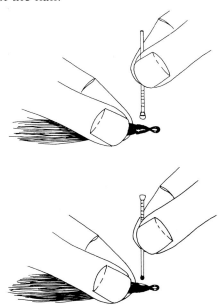

24. The finished fly.

MARABOU STREAMER

HERE IS A VERY SIMPLE MARABOU TYPE STREAMER. We show it tied with a brass wire body and with two colors of marabou for the wing. You could substitute gold tinsel or Mylar tubing for the body. The wing can be of any color, but we have found the pattern most effective when tied with a white lower wing and a black upper wing. The advantage of the brass wire body is that it adds weight to the fly, so that it will really get down in the stream. Since you are tying a streamer, you should use a long-shank hook; generally a 4X or 6X long hook is used.

We have no evidence that the painted eyes on the fly contribute to its success, but they certainly make it look better to the fisherman, and that is justification enough for putting the eyes on. If you want a really good-looking head on your streamers, you must take care when shaping it with your tying thread. If you use two or three coats of black lacquer instead of clear on the head before applying the eyes, the fly will have a really professional look.

The trick to handling the marabou is to keep it wet after cutting the fibers from the feather. The wet marabou clings together and can be handled as a single piece of material, instead of a group of soft fibers that want to go every which way.

1. Cut a 6" piece of heavy (#12) brass wire and hold it across the hook shank as shown.

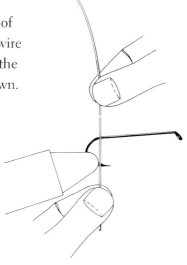

2. Hold the end of the wire that is in your left hand firmly, and wrap the wire tightly forward to a point two eyewidths back from the eye.

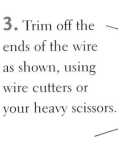

3. Trim off the ends of the wire as shown, using wire cutters or your heavy scissors.

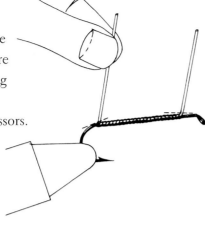

4. The finished body.

5. Attach the tying thread forward of the wire body and wrap it back to cover the end of the wire.

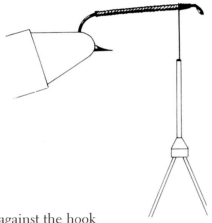

6. Cut a small patch of light-colored marabou from a marabou plume.

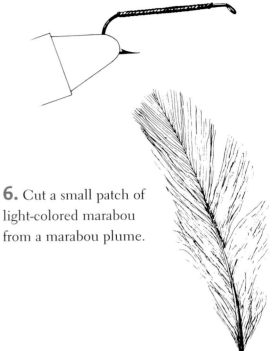

7. Measure against the hook shank: the wing should be 1¹/₂ times as long as the hook shank.

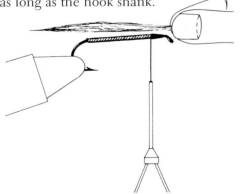

8. Tie in the marabou at the forward end of the body.

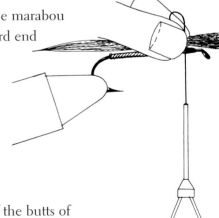

9. Trim off the butts of the marabou at an angle, as shown.

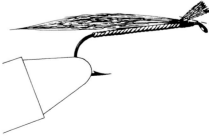

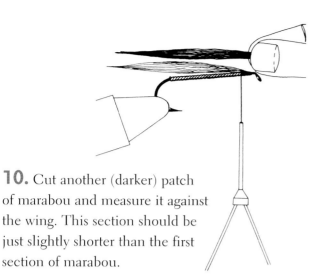

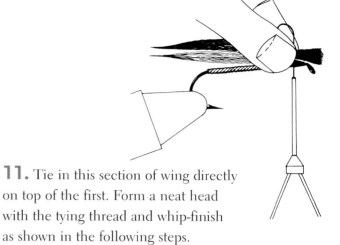

10. Cut another (darker) patch of marabou and measure it against the wing. This section should be just slightly shorter than the first section of marabou.

11. Tie in this section of wing directly on top of the first. Form a neat head with the tying thread and whip-finish as shown in the following steps.

12. Lay the first two fingers of your right hand across the thread (fingernails toward you) and wrap the thread around them as shown.

13. Rotate your hand so that your fingers are pointing up (fingernails still towards you).

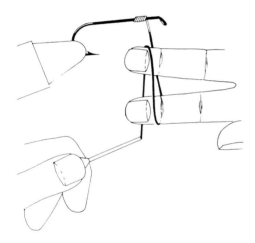

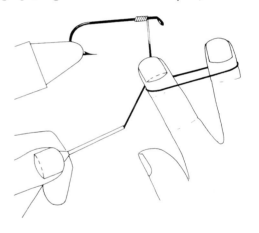

14. Raise the bobbin as you drop your middle finger.

15. Pull the slack from the loop you have formed by lowering your right hand. Grasp the rear thread with your left thumb and finger and pull downward.

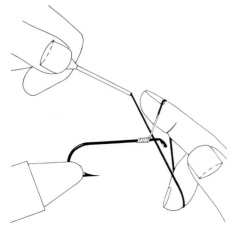

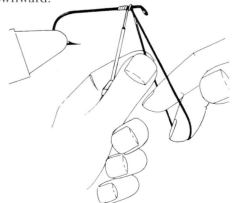

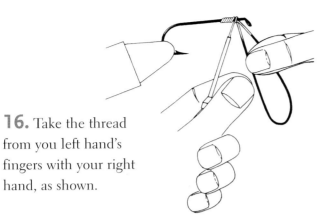

16. Take the thread from you left hand's fingers with your right hand, as shown.

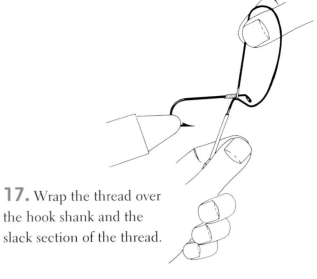

17. Wrap the thread over the hook shank and the slack section of the thread.

18. Pass the thread back to your left hand. Repeat this wrapping at least three times.

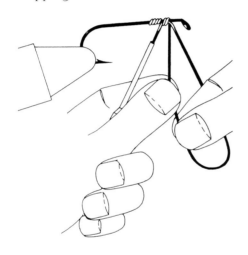

19. Pull down on the bobbin to tighten the loops around the shank and the thread. Lacquer the head.

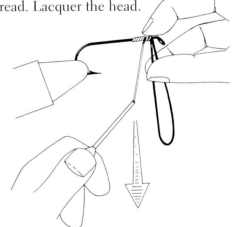

20. When the lacquer is nearly dry, apply a drop of white lacquer to each side of the head with the large end of a small finishing nail, to indicate eyes.

When the white lacquer is nearly dry, add a small dot of black lacquer using the small end of the nail.

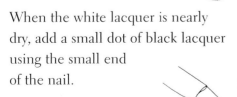

21. The finished fly.

HACKLE-WING
STREAMER

THE TYPE OF STREAMER TIED HERE USES HACKLE as the wing material. This is one area where saddle hackle really comes into its own: it gives a long, slim silhouette and moves enticingly in the water. Saddle hackle is also the best choice for the hackle at the head of the fly. You will be winding the hackle using your fingers, and the extra length found on the saddle hackle will make it easier. The pattern uses a double wing; there are two hackles tied in on each side of the hook shank. This is done so that a combination of colors can be obtained. We tie this most often using tan body floss, a yellow underwing, and a ginger overwing. The two hackles used at the head are of the same colors. Our model uses orange floss.

The four wing hackles can be tied in at one time, but it is very difficult to accomplish this so that the wings are put on straight. The easiest method is to tie in the underwings as a pair and then add the over- wings one hackle at a time, as we have shown.

To wind the two hackles at the head simultaneously, you must hold them in your fingers, because one hackle almost always will have a thicker stem than the other and will wind faster. By using your fingers instead of hackle pliers, you can allow the faster-winding hackle to slip through your fingers as you wrap.

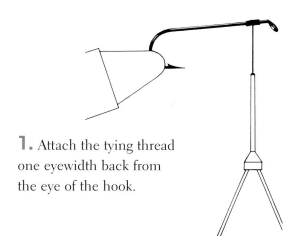

1. Attach the tying thread one eyewidth back from the eye of the hook.

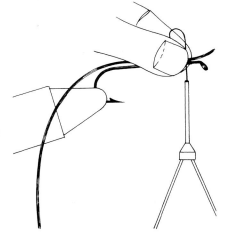

2. Tie in a 6" piece of floss.

3. Wrap the thread back to a point directly opposite the barb and then wrap it forward to the tie-in point.

4. Start wrapping the floss forward.

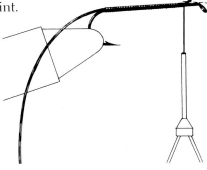

5. Your left hand stays under the hook shank— remember?

6. Wrap the floss forward and tie it down two eyewidths back from the eye.

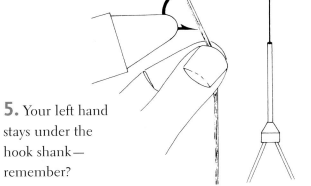

7. Measure a pair of matched hackles: the wing length should be 1½ times the length of the hook shank.

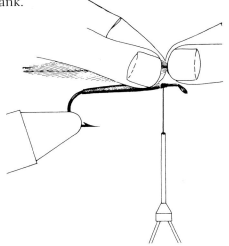

8. Trim the fibers from each side of the hackle stem and anchor the hackles on each side of the hook.

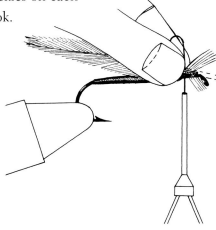

9. Prepare the third hackle in the same manner and tie it in on the back side of the hook.

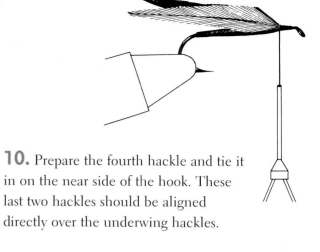

10. Prepare the fourth hackle and tie it in on the near side of the hook. These last two hackles should be aligned directly over the underwing hackles.

11. Wrap the thread to form a neat taper at the tie-in point.

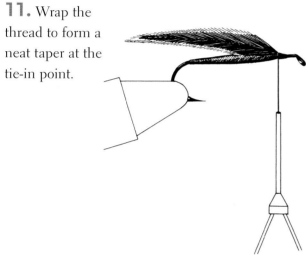

12. Select two hackles of the proper size and tie them in at the wing anchoring point.

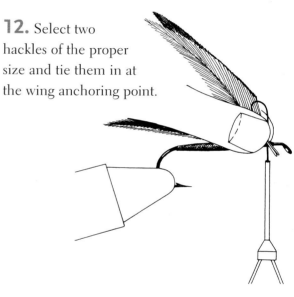

13. Cut off the hackle butts and pull the hackles upright before starting to wrap.

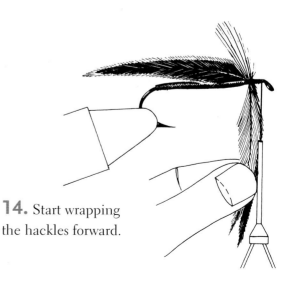

14. Start wrapping the hackles forward.

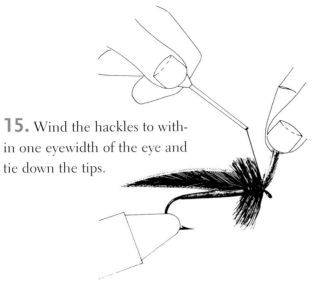

15. Wind the hackles to within one eyewidth of the eye and tie down the tips.

16. Trim off the hackle tips.

17. Lay the first two fingers of your right hand across the thread (fingernails toward you) and wrap the thread around them as shown.

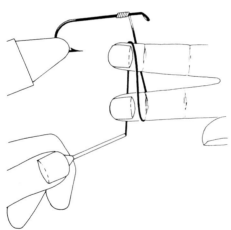

18. Rotate your hand so that your fingers are pointing up (fingernails still towards you).

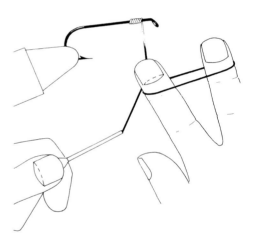

19. Raise the bobbin as you drop your middle finger.

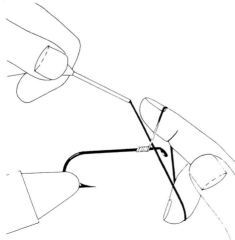

20. Pull the slack from the loop you have formed by lowering your right hand. Grasp the rear thread with your left thumb and finger and pull downward.

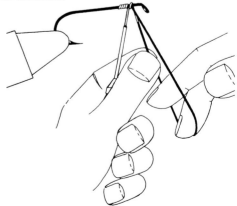

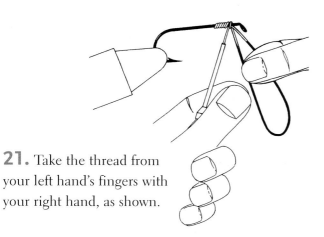

21. Take the thread from your left hand's fingers with your right hand, as shown.

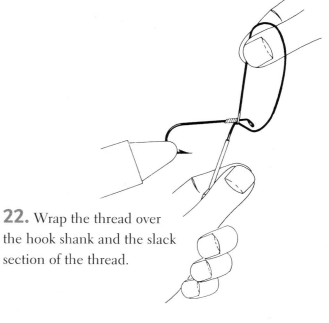

22. Wrap the thread over the hook shank and the slack section of the thread.

23. Pass the thread back to your left hand. Repeat this wrapping at least three times.

24. Pull down on the bobbin to tighten the loops around the shank and the thread. Lacquer the head.

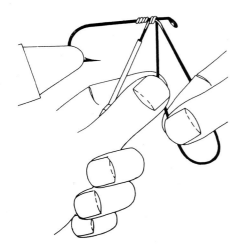

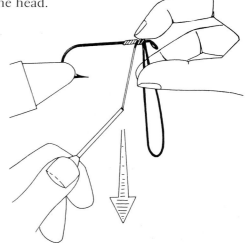

25. The finished fly.

SPUN-HAIR STREAMER (MUDDLER MINNOW)

PATTERN 18 IS AN ADAPTATION OF THE MUDDLER MINNOW; it is probably the single most useful fly that we will have you tie. When fished deep, it is a superb streamer, and if treated with floatant it is a good cricket and grasshopper imitation. The original pattern calls for a short tail of the same material as the wing, but since the technique for attaching the tail is rather difficult to teach and we don't feel that it adds to performance of the pattern, we have chosen to illustrate the pattern without it. Many patterns of this fly use squirrel tail for the first bunch of hair ahead of the wing, but we prefer it tied with deer hair so that the butts can be used as part of the trimmed deer-hair head.

The spun deer-hair head causes problems for many beginning fly-tyers and some experienced ones. First of all, the hook shank over which you are spinning the hair must be bare. Second, be sure that you get two loose wraps of thread around the bunch of hair before tightening the loop to spin the hair. There are two tricks to getting a tight, smooth surface from spun hair: (1) after spinning each bunch of hair, pack it back tightly using your thumb and fingernails; (2) singe the hair with the bottom of a match flame. This not only smoothes the hair, but also seals the ends and makes the fly more durable.

1. Attach the thread just forward of the mid-point of the hook shank and tie in a 4" piece of gold tinsel.

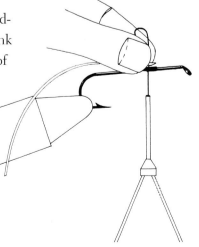

2. Begin wrapping the tinsel toward the back of the hook.

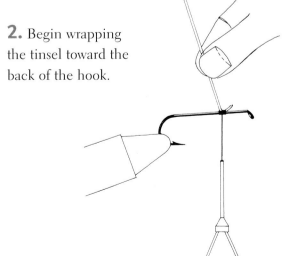

3. When a point directly opposite the barb is reached, start the tinsel forward.

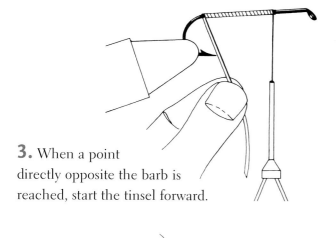

4. Wrap the tinsel toward the eye of the hook.

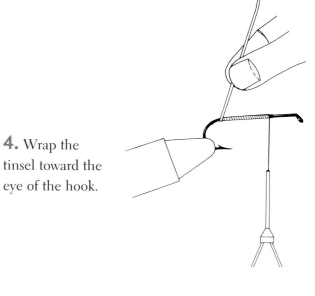

5. Tie down the end of the tinsel at the original tie-in point.

6. Trim off the excess tinsel.

7. Cut two sections of turkey quill as wide as one-third of the length of the hook shank and 1½ times as long. Attach the wings at the forward end of the body (soft-loop technique is absolutely required).

8. Trim off the butts of the wing.

9. Measure a patch of deer hair as long as from the tie-in point to the back of the hook bend.

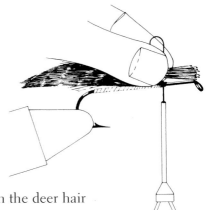

10. Tie in the deer hair just forward of the wing.

11. Trim the butts of the deer hair evenly as shown; do not trim close to the hook shank.

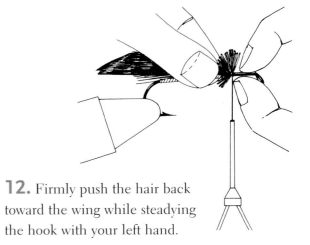

12. Firmly push the hair back toward the wing while steadying the hook with your left hand.

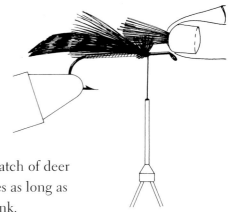

13. Cut a patch of deer hair 1$\frac{1}{2}$ times as long as the hook shank.

14. Hold the hair in place on top of the hook and make two loose wraps around it.

15. Pull firmly on the bobbin to tighten the loops and simultaneously let go of the hair so that it spins around the hook and flares out.

16. Bring the thread ahead of the hair.

17. Steadying the hook with your left hand, pack the hair back firmly with right-hand thumb and fingernails.

18. Repeat tying in hair, spinning, and packing until within one eye-width of the eye. Shape the head with your tying thread.

19. Lay the first two fingers of your right hand across the thread (fingernails toward you) and wrap the thread around them as shown.

20. Rotate your hand so that your fingers are pointing up (fingernails still towards you).

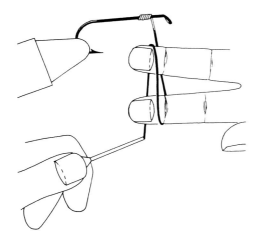

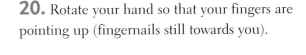

21. Raise the bobbin as you drop your middle finger.

22. Pull the slack from the loop you have formed by lowering your right hand. Grasp the rear thread with your left thumb and finger and pull downward.

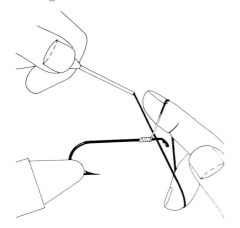

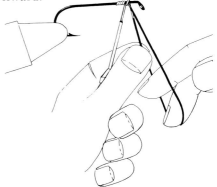

23. Take the thread from your left hand's fingers with your right hand, as shown.

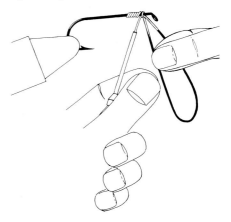

24. Wrap the thread over the hook shank and the slack section of the thread.

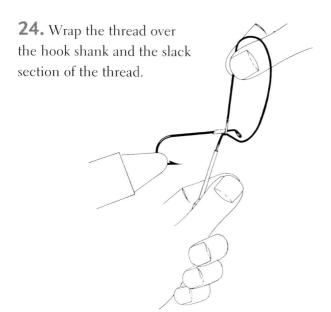

25. Pass the thread back to your left hand. Repeat this wrapping at least three times.

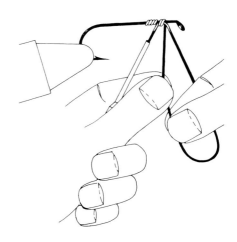

26. Pull down on the bobbin to tighten the loops around the shank and the thread. Lacquer the head.

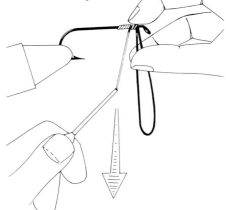

27. Trim the head to shape as shown and singe it with the bottom edge of a match flame to smoothen the deer hair.

28. Use the match flame to shape the head as shown.

29. The finished fly.

PATTERN
19

HUMPY
VARIATION

THE PATTERN THAT WE ARE GOING TO HAVE YOU TIE NEXT is one of the most used patterns in the western United States. It is one of the many variations of the hair-bodied flies called Humpies. Of all the dry flies in my fly boxes, this is my favorite. It is not a particularly good imitation of any insect, although its upright wing would suggest a mayfly. However, this fly will float through really rough water where you would drown a normal dry fly in seconds, and that may be its secret—it simply allows us to float a fly where we otherwise wouldn't be able to. Also, in the really heavy, fast water the trout doesn't get as good a look at the imitation because the fly is traveling fast and the ruffled surface of the water distorts its view.

The only thing a little difficult about tying the pattern is getting the hair the right length, since it is used as both the body and the wing. The length of the hair should be equal to the distance from the eye to the back of the tail.

1. Attach the tying thread at the position shown.

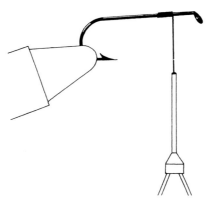

2. Cut a small bunch of dark elk hair and even the ends by using some form of hair stacker.

3. Measure the length of the evened hair to equal the distance from the back of the eye to the back of the bend.

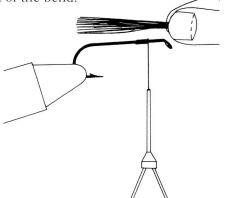

4. Tie in the tail and wrap back to the start of the bend. Trim off the hair butts.

5. Measure a length of lighter elk hair against the hook. The length should be equal to the distance from the back of the eye to the end of the tail.

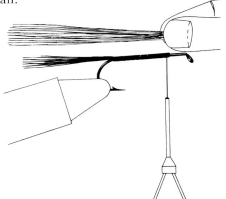

6. Tie in the hair at the forward end of the thread wraps.

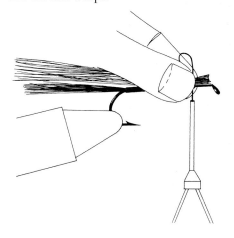

7. Spiral the thread back over the hair to the start of the bend. Trim off the hair butts.

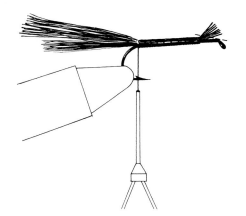

8. Spiral the thread forward to the tie-in point.

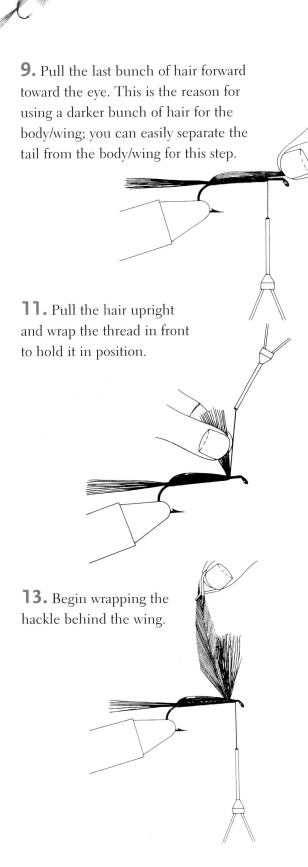

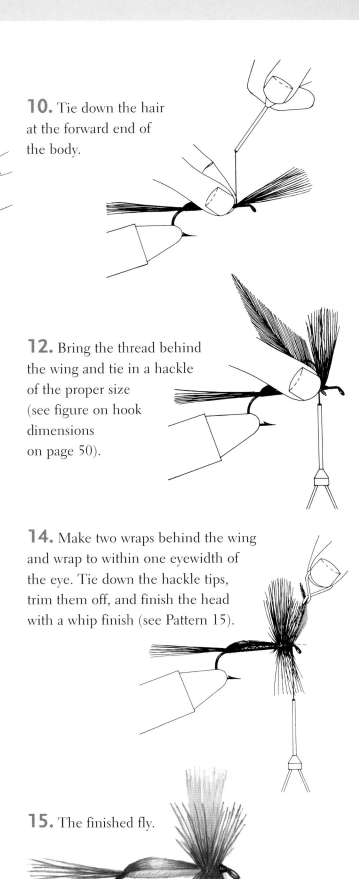

9. Pull the last bunch of hair forward toward the eye. This is the reason for using a darker bunch of hair for the body/wing; you can easily separate the tail from the body/wing for this step.

10. Tie down the hair at the forward end of the body.

11. Pull the hair upright and wrap the thread in front to hold it in position.

12. Bring the thread behind the wing and tie in a hackle of the proper size (see figure on hook dimensions on page 50).

13. Begin wrapping the hackle behind the wing.

14. Make two wraps behind the wing and wrap to within one eyewidth of the eye. Tie down the hackle tips, trim them off, and finish the head with a whip finish (see Pattern 15).

15. The finished fly.

SHRIMP OR SCUD (GAMMARUS)

SHOW THIS PATTERN TO MOST FLY-FISHERS AND THEY WILL TELL YOU that it is a shrimp imitation, and indeed it could be, but since freshwater shrimp are not very prevalent, it is probably more often taken by the trout to be a scud (Gammarus). Since we are again simulating an underwater animal (a crustacean in this case), we want to tie this pattern on a wet-fly hook, and since scuds are relatively short, a regular-length hook will work very well. If you want to get a realistic shape to this imitation, most of the hook manufacturers make hooks with a special shape just to use for patterns of this type.

We tie this pattern in two colors: light tan with salmon-colored tail and hackle, and gray with dark- gray tail and hackle. Dark olive would also be a good choice, since some of the scuds are in this color range.

1. Attach the thread as shown and trim off the tag end.

2. Measure a bunch of soft hackle fibers for the tail; they should reach from the back of the eye to the back of the hook's bend.

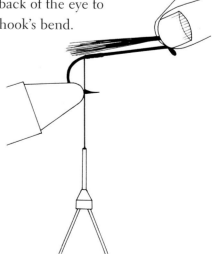

3. Position the fibers at the tie-in point and pass them to your left hand.

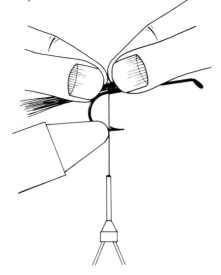

4. Tie in the tail fibers.

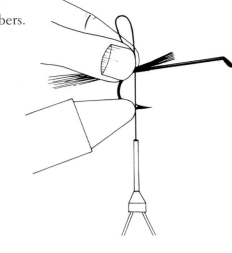

5. Trim off the fiber butts.

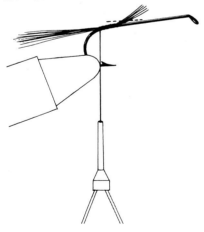

6. Apply dubbing to the thread.

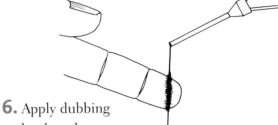

7. Begin wrapping the dubbed body. You will have to apply dubbing several times to wrap the whole body.

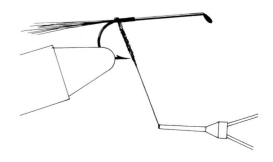

8. Wrap to within one eyewidth of the eye.

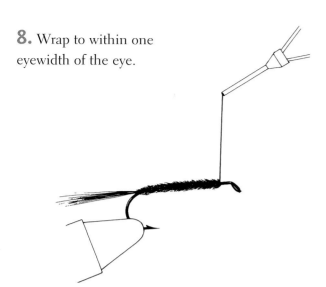

9. Run the tying thread to the eye and back to the forward end of the body.

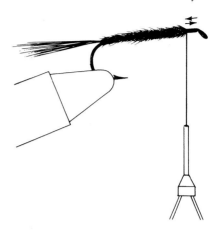

10. Invert the hook in the vise.

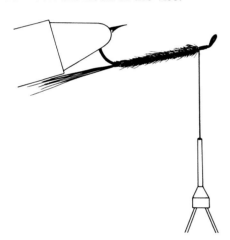

11. Measure a bunch of soft hackle fibers for the throat. The fibers should extend from the tie-in point to the tip of the hook point.

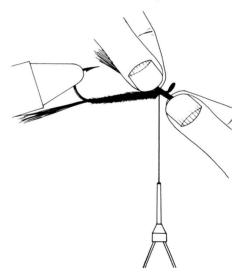

12. Place the fibers in position so that about one-half are on either side of the eye, and tie down.

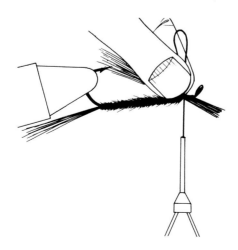

13. Pull the butts of the hackle fibers toward the rear of the hook.

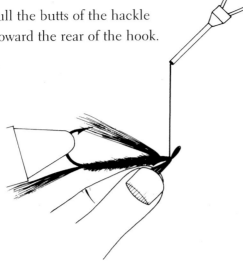

14. Wrap back on the fiber butts as shown.

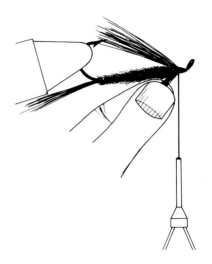

15. Finish the head of the fly and trim the hackle butts as illustrated.

16. The finished fly.

SIMPLE WET-FLY ATTRACTOR

THE REMAINING PATTERNS THAT WE ARE GOING TO SHOW YOU are a mix of attractors and flies that require some more-specialized techniques. They will also serve as a review of the steps we have covered in presenting the first 20 flies.

The first attractor pattern is a very simple wet-fly pattern that may be effective as a pupal imitation, or perhaps as an emerger. It should be tied on a wet-fly hook of standard length. Our model was tied with hackle and peacock herl.

Your technique should be developed well enough by now that you are starting to pay close attention to detail; proportion, neatness, and the finishing of the head in a precise manner are the hallmarks of a good fly-tyer.

1. Start the thread attachment one eyewidth back from the eye.

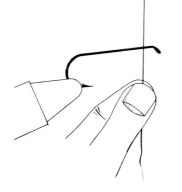

2. Wrap the thread back over itself to the point shown and trim off the excess.

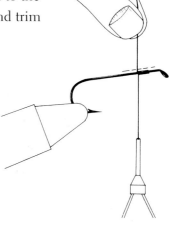

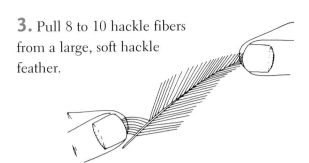

3. Pull 8 to 10 hackle fibers from a large, soft hackle feather.

4. Measure the hackle fibers against the hook shank; the fibers should reach from the back of the eye to the back of the hook bend.

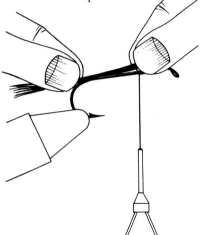

5. Holding the fibers at the measured point, move the fibers back to the start of the hook bend.

6. Grasp the hackle fibers at the bend with your left hand and move your right hand forward to the tie-in point.

7. Hold the fibers at the tie-in point with your right hand.

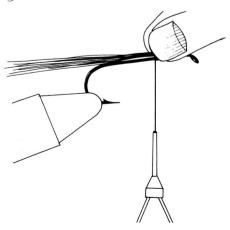

8. Grasp the fibers and the hook shank with your left hand as shown.

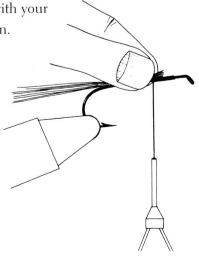

9. Tie down the butts of the fibers using the soft loop.

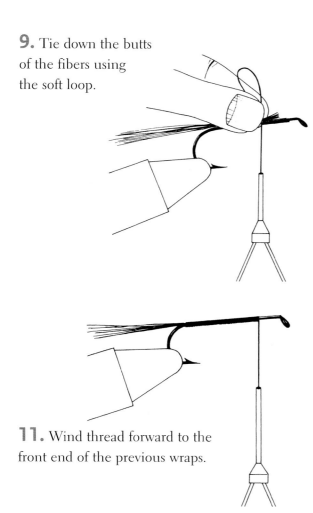

10. Wrap the thread back to a point directly opposite the barb of the hook. To keep the tail material on the top of the hook shank as you wrap, hold the fibers offset toward you as you wrap and allow the thread to carry the tail to the top.

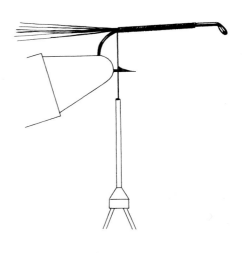

11. Wind thread forward to the front end of the previous wraps.

12. Hold two pieces of peacock herl on the top of the shank and tie them in, using the soft loop.

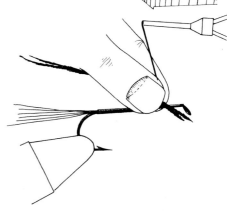

13. Remember: to tie the soft loop you must first bring the thread back between the thumb and finger to form the loop and then pull straight down with the bobbin while holding the material firmly in place.

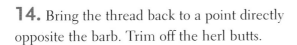

14. Bring the thread back to a point directly opposite the barb. Trim off the herl butts.

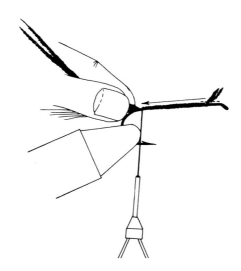

15. Wind the thread forward to the front of the previous wraps.

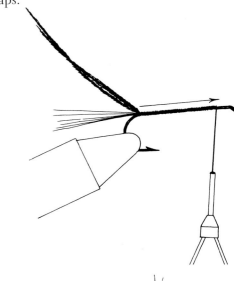

16. Start winding the herl forward with your right hand.

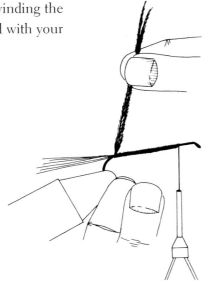

17. Don't forget that your left hand should remain under the hook as the right hand does the actual wrapping.

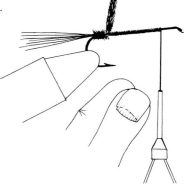

18. Wrap the herl forward to the front of the thread wraps.

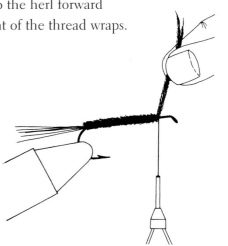

19. Hold the tips in your right hand and the bobbin in your left hand.

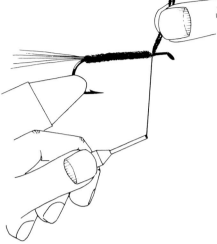

20. Pass the bobbin over the top of the hook and drop it on the back side to tie down the herl.

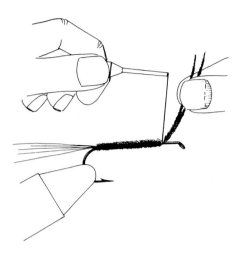

21. Trim off the herl tips.

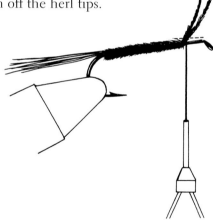

22. Wrap the thread forward to just behind the eye.

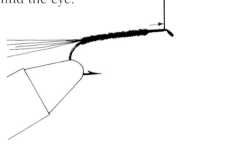

23. Wrap the thread back to the forward end of the body.

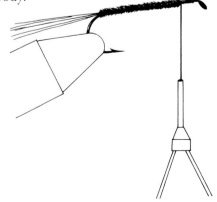

24. Tie in a hackle of the proper size at the forward end of the body.

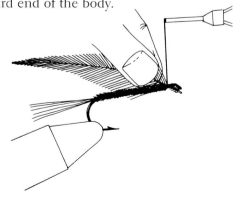

25. Trim off the hackle butt.

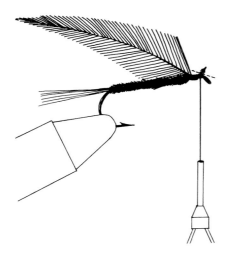

26. Begin winding the hackle forward.

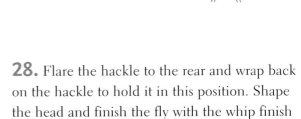

27. Wrap the hackle to within one eyewidth of the eye, tie it down, and trim off the tips.

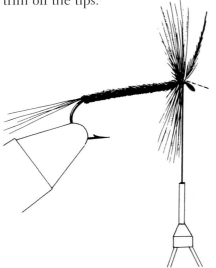

28. Flare the hackle to the rear and wrap back on the hackle to hold it in this position. Shape the head and finish the fly with the whip finish (see Pattern 15).

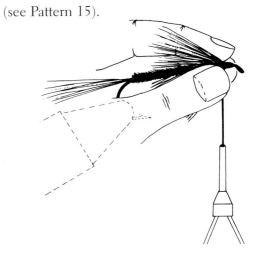

29. The finished fly.

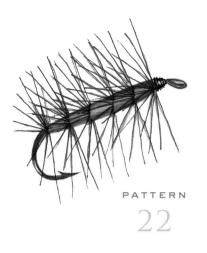

Dry-Fly
Attractor

THIS IS A DRY-FLY ATTRACTOR PATTERN OF THE PALMERED TYPE. We show it tied with a floss body—as it is for the Bloody Butcher (red floss with black hackle) and the Orange Asher (orange floss with ginger hackle)—but the same pattern tied on a long shank hook with a chenille body is a Woolly Worm. The color combinations that you might use are endless. Flies tied in this manner are very good floaters because of the large amount of hackle used. They can be deadly when caterpillars abound.

1. Attach the thread an eyewidth back from the eye and wrap back to the start of the bend. Tie in a hackle of the proper size.

2. Advance the thread to the front of the thread wraps.

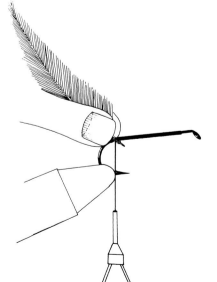

3. Tie in a piece of floss.

4. Wrap the thread back to the rear of the body.

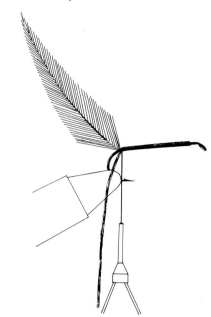

5. Advance the thread forward again.

6. Begin wrapping the floss forward.

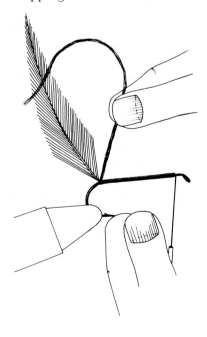

7. Wrap the floss to the forward end of the body, tie it down, and trim off the excess.

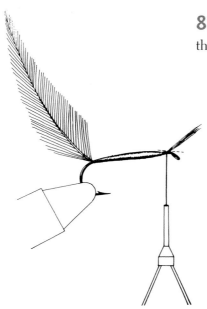

8. Begin winding the hackle forward.

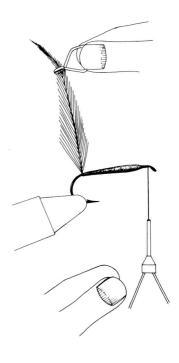

9. Wind the hackle in a spiral as you advance toward the front of the hook.

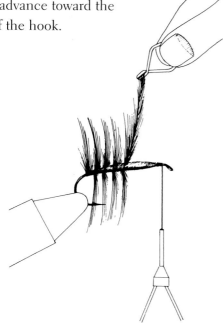

10. Tie down the hackle and cut off the tip. Form a neat head and tie off the fly with a whip finish (see Pattern 15).

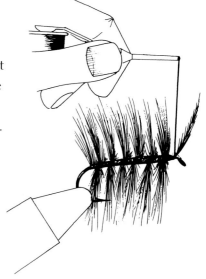

11. The finished fly.

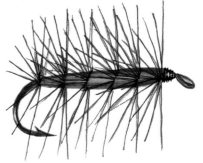

WET-FLY ATTRACTOR
(RIO GRANDE KING)

HERE IS ANOTHER WET-FLY PATTERN THAT IS A REALLY GOOD PRODUCER in the western United States. It is called a Rio Grande King and is probably effective because it has the shape of an emerging insect.

There are two things you should learn from tying Pattern 23. First, notice that the chenille being used for the body has all of the fuzz removed from the center thread at the end, so that you can attach it by its thread, and thus you won't create a lump when you start wrapping. Second, pay close attention to the steps involved in preparing the calf tail for the wing. Calf tail is very curly and doesn't lend itself well to the use of a hair stacker. The method shown is about the only way to get the hair ends even.

1. Start the thread attachment one eyewidth back from the eye.

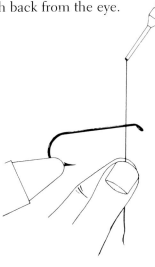

2. Wrap the thread back over itself to the point shown and trim off the excess.

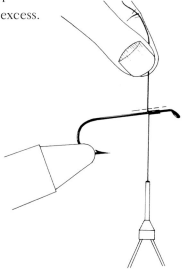

3. Pull 8 to 10 hackle fibers from a large, soft hackle feather.

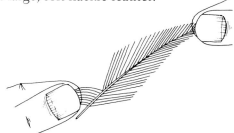

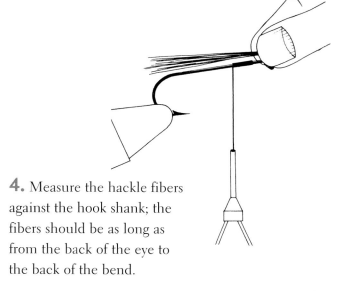

4. Measure the hackle fibers against the hook shank; the fibers should be as long as from the back of the eye to the back of the bend.

5. Holding the fibers at the measured point, move the fibers back to the start of the hook bend.

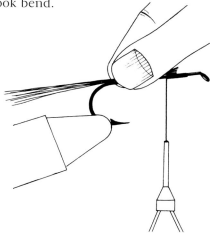

6. Grasp the hackle fibers at the bend with your left hand and move your right hand forward to the tie-in point.

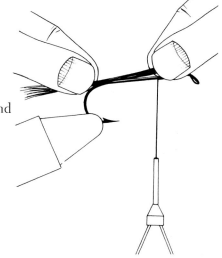

7. Hold the fibers at the tie-in point with your right hand.

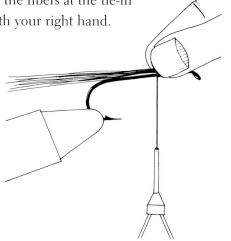

8. Grasp the fibers and the hook shank with your left hand as shown.

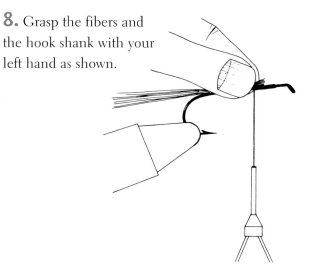

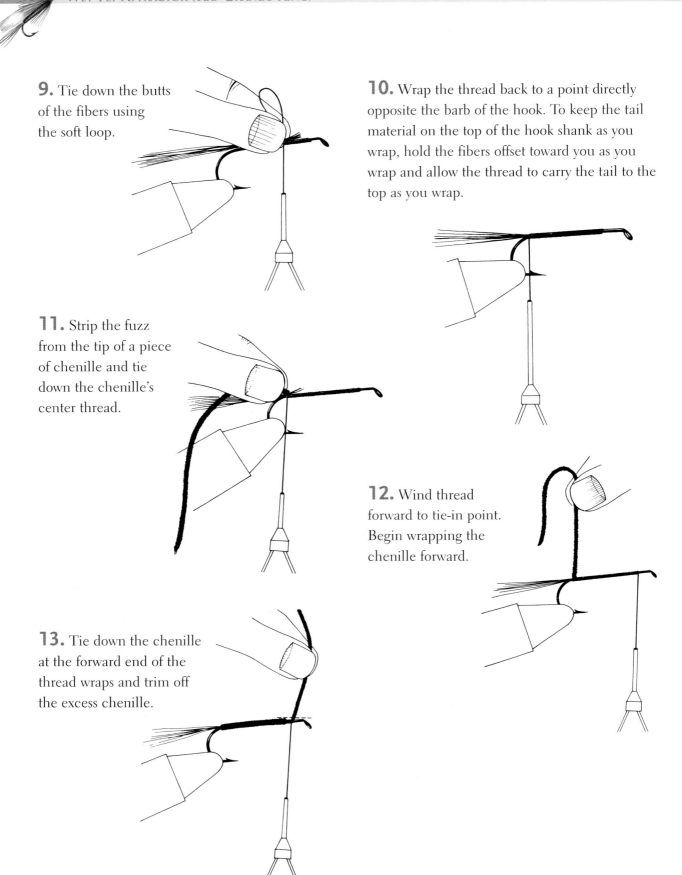

9. Tie down the butts of the fibers using the soft loop.

10. Wrap the thread back to a point directly opposite the barb of the hook. To keep the tail material on the top of the hook shank as you wrap, hold the fibers offset toward you as you wrap and allow the thread to carry the tail to the top as you wrap.

11. Strip the fuzz from the tip of a piece of chenille and tie down the chenille's center thread.

12. Wind thread forward to tie-in point. Begin wrapping the chenille forward.

13. Tie down the chenille at the forward end of the thread wraps and trim off the excess chenille.

14. Cut off and discard the very tip and butt of a calf tail. Cut a small bunch of hair from the remaining portion.

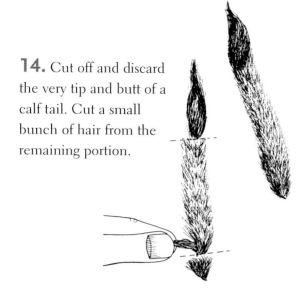

15. Hold the tips of the hair in your left hand and pull out the short hairs with your right hand.

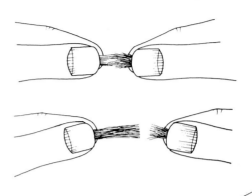

16. Hold the butts in your right hand and pull out the long hairs with your left hand.

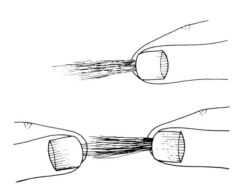

17. Measure the wing length. The hairs should extend from the tie-in point to the midpoint of the tail.

18. Tie in the wing and trim off the hair butts.

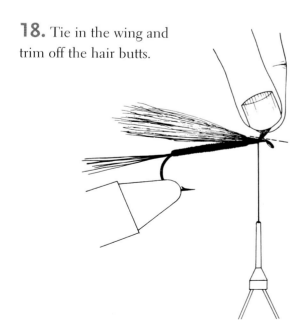

19. Tie in a hackle of the proper size.

20. Begin winding the hackle forward.

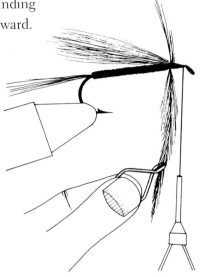

21. Wind the hackle to within one eyewidth of the eye and tie down the tip.

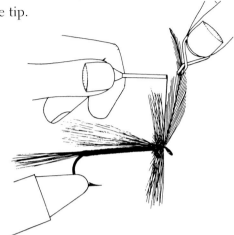

22. Cut off the hackle tip.

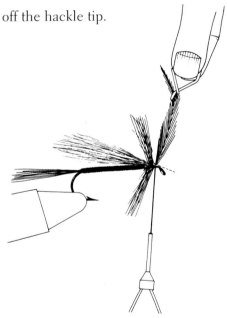

23. Flare the hackle to the rear and wrap back on it to hold it in this position. Finish the head of the fly.

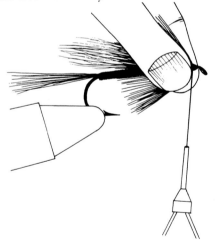

24. The finished fly.

WET-FLY ATTRACTOR (SALMON-FLY TYPE)

WE HAVE CHOSEN PATTERN 24 BECAUSE ITS SIMPLICITY has a certain delicacy that is more difficult to achieve than it would seem. Much like the classic salmon flies, this fly requires perfect proportion of materials and flawless execution of technique to be tied properly. In short, it's meant as a bit of a self-test for you to see how you are progressing.

Pay particular attention to the taper of the body. This has been shown in many of the previous patterns, but we doubt that you made a concerted effort to imitate it; very few students do until later in the learning process. The method of accomplishing the taper is to start winding the floss flat on the hook shank at the tail and then begin overlapping the floss wraps as you advance forward, much as you did earlier on the rubber band bodied stonefly nymph.

The flaring of the hackle toward the rear of the hook is another detail that is sometimes hard to get. Yet this detail counts a lot toward the appearance of the finished fly. To get the desired even flare, try wetting your finger and thumb before pulling the hackle to the rear. Start with your thumb and finger in front of, and slightly below, the eye, and then follow the shape of the hook with your thumb and finger. Your finger and thumb should move slightly upward along the eye and then toward the rear and down, following the hook shank, as the hackle fibers are picked up and swept back.

1. Start the thread attachment one eyewidth back from the eye.

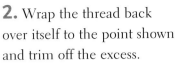

2. Wrap the thread back over itself to the point shown and trim off the excess.

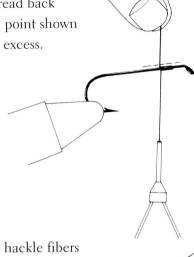

3. Pull 8 to 10 hackle fibers from a large, soft hackle feather.

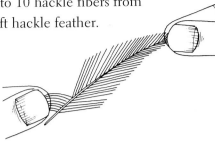

4. Measure the hackle fibers against the hook shank; the fibers should be as long as the distance from the back of the eye to the back of the bend.

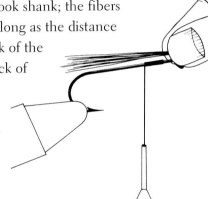

5. Holding the fibers at the measured point, move the fibers back to the start of the hook bend.

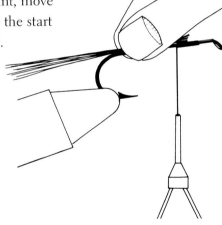

6. Grasp the hackle fibers at the bend with your left hand and move your right hand forward to the tie-in point.

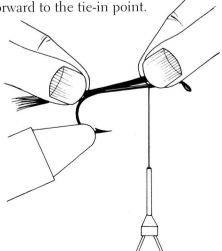

7. Hold the fibers at the tie-in point with your right hand.

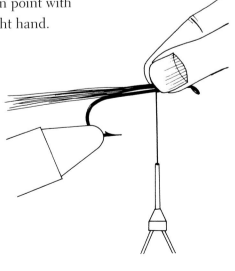

8. Grasp the fibers and the hook shank with your left hand as shown.

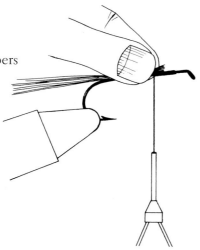

9. Tie down the butts of the fibers using the soft loop.

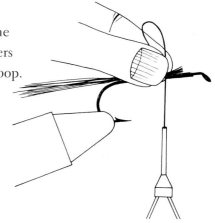

10. Tie in a piece of tinsel at the forward end of the thread wraps.

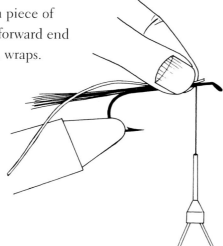

11. Wrap back on the tinsel and tail as shown.

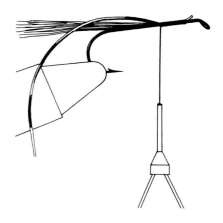

12. Tie in a piece of floss at the rear point of the previous wraps.

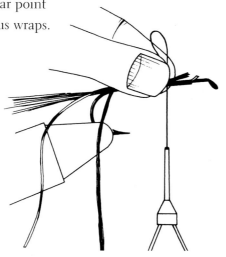

13. Wrap over the floss, tail, and tinsel to the start of the bend. Notice how smooth the thread wrap is; that's the reason for tying in the materials as we did—to avoid making lumps.

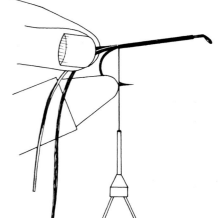

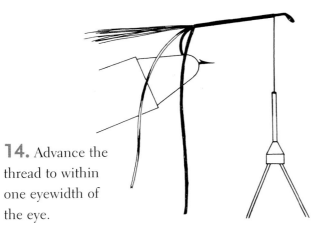

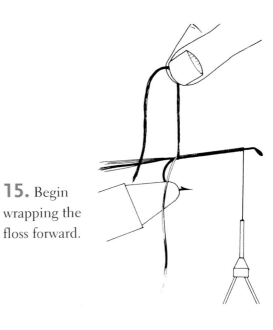

14. Advance the thread to within one eyewidth of the eye.

15. Begin wrapping the floss forward.

16. Remember to start overlapping the floss as you move forward, to get the desired taper to the body.

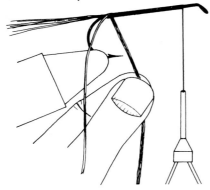

17. Tie down the floss and trim off the excess.

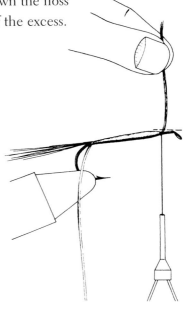

18. Start winding the tinsel forward in a spiral.

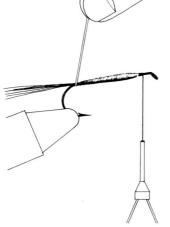

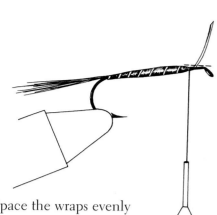

19. Space the wraps evenly as you come forward. Tie down the tinsel and trim it.

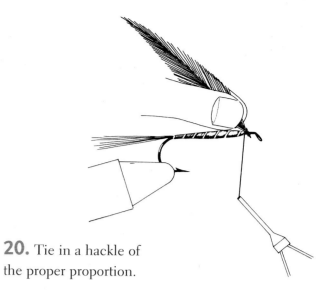

20. Tie in a hackle of the proper proportion.

21. Wrap four turns of the hackle forward, tie down the tips, and trim off the excess.

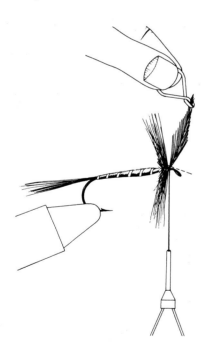

22. Flare the hackle to the rear and wind back on it to hold it in position. Make a neat head and finish it with the whip finish (see Pattern 15).

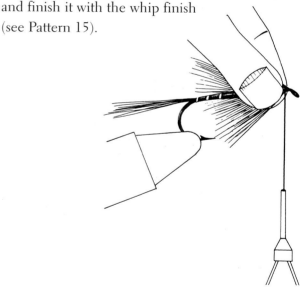

23. The finished fly.

MATUKA

THE MATUKA IS A VERY OLD STYLE OF FLY, whose popularity returned when it was reintroduced by Swisher and Richards in their book *Fly Fishing Strategy.* A singular advantage of the Matuka tie is that the wing will not become tangled around the bend of the hook as regular hackle wings often do. The pattern also provides a good minnow silhouette, and the tail provides very good action. The Matuka is a good producer as well as being interesting to tie.

1. Attach the tying thread two eyewidths back of the eye.

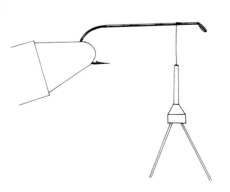

2. Tie in a 6" piece of fine copper or brass wire.

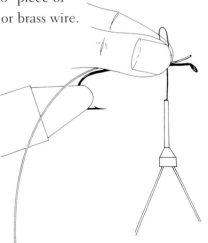

3. Wrap the thread back over the wire to a point directly opposite the point of the barb.

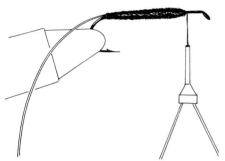

4. Dub the tying thread with a natural or synthetic dubbing. (See Pattern 2 for a detailed explanation of how to dub.)

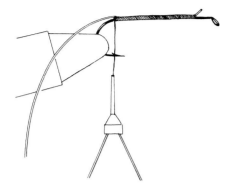

5. Wrap forward with the thread to the initial tie-in point.

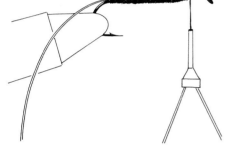

6. A. Select a matched pair of soft, webby hackles. Position them with concave sides together as shown. B. Tear the fibers from the bottom edges of both hackles, as illustrated. C. The paired hackles should fit the hook length as shown.

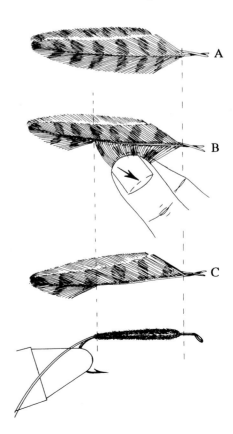

7. Tie in the paired hackles at the original tie-in point.

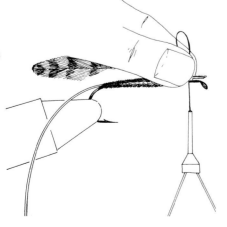

8. Trim off the hackle stems.

9. Start wrapping the wire by coming under the hook towards yourself.

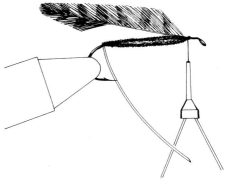

10. Hold the tail section of the hackles firmly with your left hand. Wet your right thumb and first finger and stroke the hackle forward to leave a gap between the fibers, as shown.

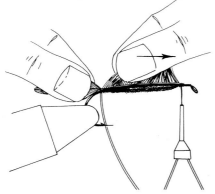

11. Wrap the wire over the top of both the hackle stem and the hook shank while holding the hackles in place with your left hand. Bring the wire down under the hook shank, spiraling forward.

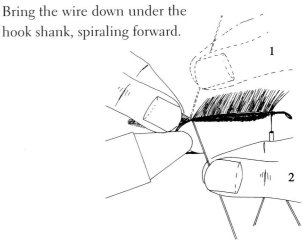

12. Keeping the tension on the wire with your right hand, use your dubbing needle to separate another section of fibers; sweep the section to the rear with your left hand.

13. Hold the rear section of fibers in your left hand and bring the wire up over the hackle stems and the hook shank. Bring the wire down under the hook shank, and spiral the wire forward one turn.

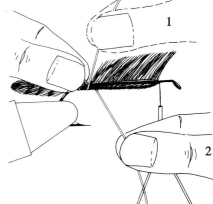

14. Hold the tension on the wire with your right hand, and use your dubbing needle in your left hand to separate another section of fibers; sweep the section to the rear.

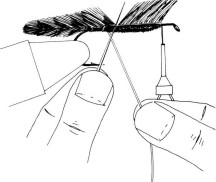

15. Continue working forward by repeating steps 12 and 13 until the wire reaches the original tie-in point. Tie down the wire and trim off the excess wire.

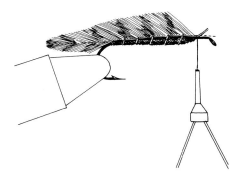

16. Select a soft, webby hackle and tie it in at the original tie-in point.

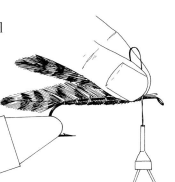

17. Trim off the hackle butt.

18. Wind the hackle forward to just behind the eye, tie it down, and trim off the tip.

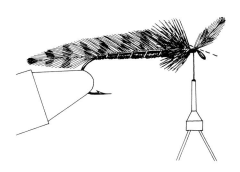

19. Flare the hackle to the rear, form a neat head, and whip finish it (see Pattern 15).

ZONKER

HERE'S ANOTHER STREAMER PATTERN THAT IS A GREAT PRODUCER. It's called a Zonker. It was developed by a good friend of ours, Dan Byford. At first glance, the wing would suggest that this is another Matuka pattern, but on the Zonker the wing is a narrow strip of rabbit hide with its fur on. The rabbit fur provides a bulkier body than the hackle wing on the Matuka does, but it still provides motion and animation. The tubular Mylar body insures that the Zonker has the flash of a real minnow. This pattern is a steady producer for us; we suggest that you keep a few in sizes #8 through #14 in your vest.

1. Attach the tying thread at a point directly opposite the point of the barb.

2. Cut off a length of Mylar tubing a little longer than the full length of the hook and remove its cotton core. Use your bodkin to separate the strands of Mylar to the length shown.

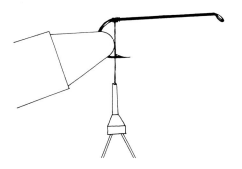

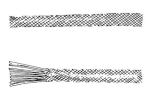

3. Slide the tube over the hook shank from the front of the hook.

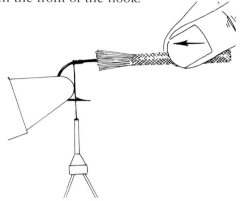

4. Position the tube as shown. Note that the unraveled length of the tube extends from opposite the point of the barb to about one eyewidth back from the eye.

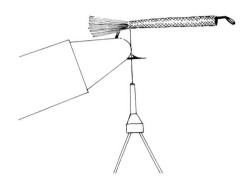

5. Hold the "tail" (the separated strands) with your left hand and tie down the back end of the tube.

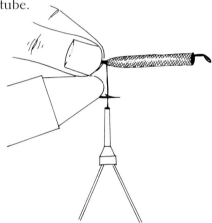

6. Whip finish and cut off the thread. (See Pattern 15 for whip-finishing instructions.)

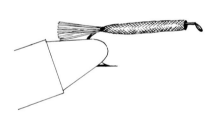

7. Pull the front end of the tube back as shown.

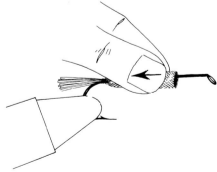

8. Reattach the tying thread one eyewidth back from the eye.

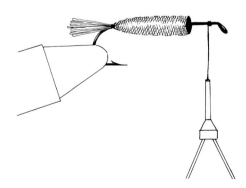

9. Slide the tube forward again and, holding it firmly in place with your left hand, wrap over the forward end, whip finish, and cut away the thread.

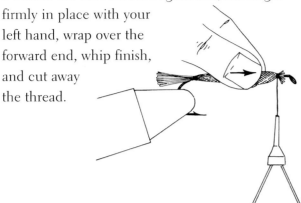

10. Trim off the ends of the Mylar near the eye.

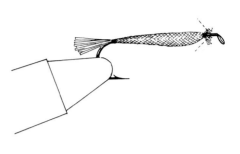

11. Reattach the thread at the rear of the hook. Cut a section of your rabbit hide strip to the length shown.

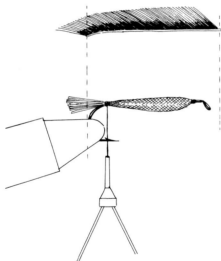

12. Separate the hair so that the section from the curve of the hook back is in your left hand. Holding the strip in place, anchor it firmly, using the soft-loop technique and wrapping the thread where the hair separates.

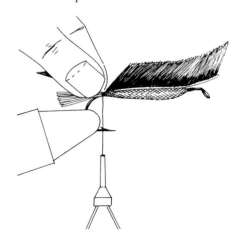

13. Whip finish it neatly and trim off the end of the thread.

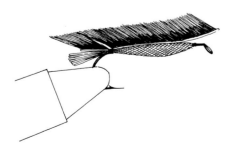

14. Reattach the tying thread at the original tie-in point at the front of the hook. Separate the hair from the tie-in forward, as shown.

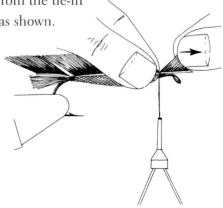

15. Holding the strip firmly with your right hand, anchor the strip firmly with thread, using soft loops.

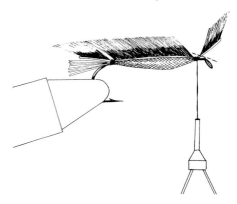

16. Trim off the excess fur strip, as shown.

17. Invert the hook in the vise. Pull out 10 to 12 soft hackle fibers from a large hackle.

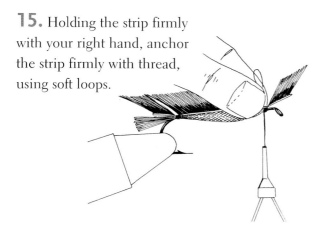

18. Hold the hackle fibers in place with your left hand and anchor them, using the soft-loop technique.

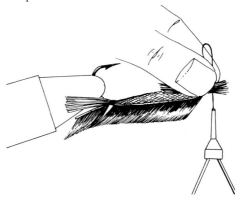

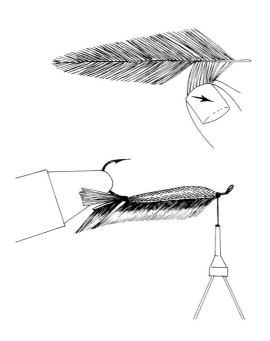

19. Place the hook upright in the vise, form a neat head, and whip-finish the thread (see Pattern 15).

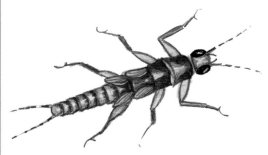

GOLDEN
STONEFLY NYMPH

THE GOLDEN STONEFLY NYMPH IS A BIT COMPLICATED, but it is not difficult; it just has many steps. It's well worth the effort though, because this is as effective an imitation as we have found. Colors can be chosen to match any of the stonefly nymphs; tan, brown, nearly black, olive, and amber are all good choices, depending on the insects found in the streams that you frequent.

Don called one early spring day to tell me that the fishing was pretty hot down on the Arkansas River and that the trout were really turned on to stonefly nymphs. The predominant stonefly in the stretches where we fish is the golden stonefly *(Acroneuria californica)*, so I tied up a few using a bright yellow yarn and ribbed it with a clear, light brown Swannundaze. They were very pretty but seemed awfully bright, even to represent the amber-colored stonefly. Don scoffed a bit when I showed him what I had brought along. He had a similar tie, but it was much more subdued in its coloration. My son, Lance, and I started taking trout immediately, and, although Don was picking up a fish now and then, the Golden Stonefly was getting takes at least two to one over Don's pattern.

If you hear Don tell the story, he nearly drowned getting down on his knees in the middle of the Arkansas to beg for a fly. To set the record straight, I didn't make him get down on his knees and only insisted that he grovel for a couple of minutes before I gave him one. We caught a lot of trout that day. After taking enough to be satisfied for a while, we began plucking rocks from the stream bed to see if there was any explanation for the success of these very brightly colored flies. Sure enough, we found a scattering of stoneflies that were almost entirely a bright buttercup yellow. We called our friend Gary LaFontaine, who cleared up the question for us. It seems that as the nymph grows, it keeps outgrowing its exoskeleton, therefore it sheds it (molts). The bright yellow nymphs we were finding were those who were in the instar or stage before their new exoskeletons had formed. We think that the bright color of the insect in this stage makes it more noticeable to the trout and, therefore, acts as a trigger to the fish that this is food. Needless to say, we always have some of these along in bright yellow!

1. Attach the thread two eyewidths back of the eye.

2. Wrap the thread back to be opposite the point of the barb and dub a short section of thread.

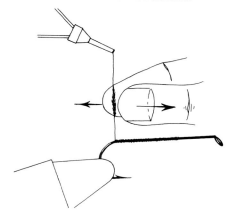

3. Wrap the dubbed thread to form a small ball at the rear of the body; then wrap the thread forward to about the midpoint of the shank.

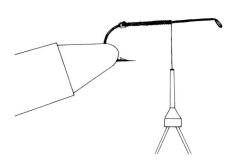

4. To make the tail, select two stiff moose mane hairs, even out their tips, and tie them in, using a soft loop. The hairs should extend beyond the hook curve, as shown.

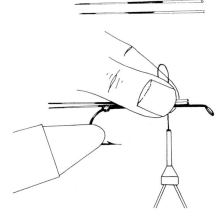

5. Use your thumbnail to press the hairs down to either side of the hook's bend, as shown.

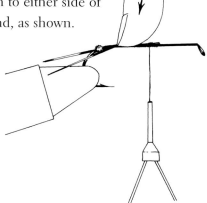

6. Hold the hairs with your left hand so that one is on each side of the hook's bend.

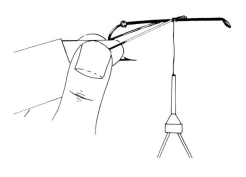

7. Wrap back on the hair butts to just behind the dubbed ball.

8. The tail should end up positioned as Don shows it here (overhead view).

9. Wrap the thread forward to the hook's midpoint and tie in a 6" piece of ribbing material (Swannundaze, flat monofilament, or Larva Lace).

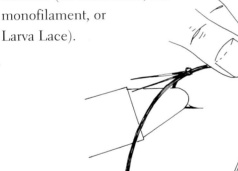

10. Tie in a 6" piece of yarn at the same place you tied the ribbing material.

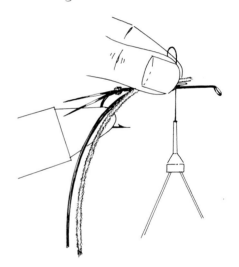

11. With your thread, wrap back on both the yarn and the ribbing material to just behind the dubbed ball; then wrap back up to the hook's midpoint.

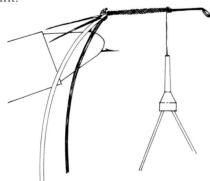

12. Wrap the yarn forward, tie it down, and trim off the excess yarn.

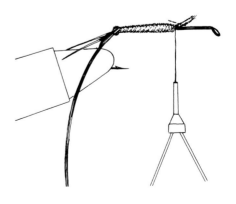

13. Spiral the ribbing forward, tie it down, and trim off the excess ribbing.

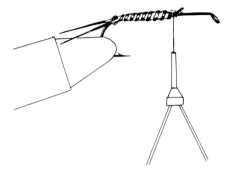

14. Wrap the thread back on the yarn 3 or 4 turns and then tie in a narrow piece of Swiss Straw.

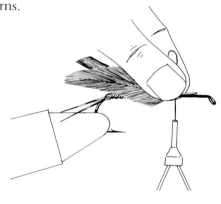

15. Wrap a few turns forward with the thread and then back as shown. Trim off the excess Swiss Straw near the eye.

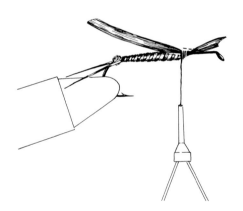

16. Tie in a soft hackle behind the thread turns.

17. Wrap back on the hackle stem with thread.

18. Dub a section of thread rather heavily, and wind it forward to one eyewidth behind the eye.

19. Palmer the hackle forward, tie it down, and trim off the hackle tip.

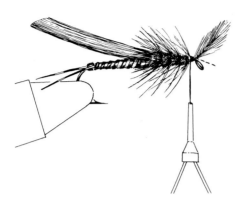

20. Fold the Swiss Straw forward over the hackle and tie down. Don't trim off the excess yet.

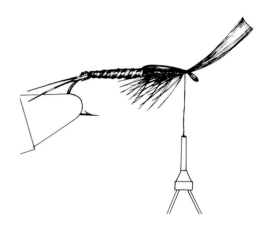

21. Fold the Swiss Straw back towards the rear of the hook and lay your dubbing needle across it. Now fold the Swiss Straw forward over the eye of the hook as shown and tie it down again. Trim off the excess Swiss Straw. Form a neat head and whip finish it (see Pattern 15).

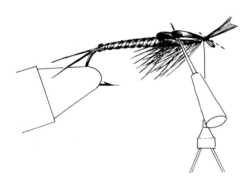

22. With the hook still in the vise, pull the eye towards you a bit to offset the hook point (see overhead view, top). Then remove it from the vise and, holding it as shown, bend a slight hump in the shank to provide a more realistic shape to the fly.

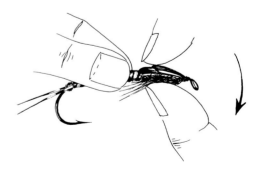

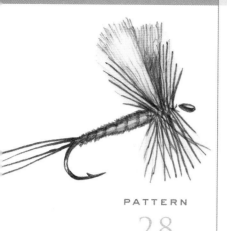

MAYFLY ADULT WITH POLYPROPYLENE WING

THIS POLY YARN DRY FLY IS ONE OF MY FAVORITES. The polypropylene wing is extremely durable, provides a good mayfly silhouette, and is easy to tie, especially in the really small sizes. The wing type can, of course, be matched up with your choice of dry-fly tailing method and body type. We carry these with us in a full range of sizes, from #12 clear down to #22, in gray, tan, dun, and olive. If I had to be restricted to only one mayfly adult pattern type, this would be my choice.

1. Attach tying thread two eyewidths back from the eye.

2. Strip off 6 to 8 fibers from a stiff dry-fly hackle.

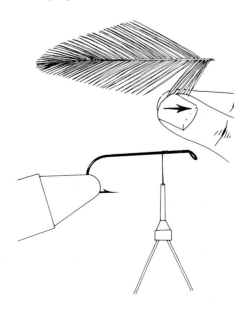

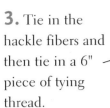

3. Tie in the hackle fibers and then tie in a 6" piece of tying thread.

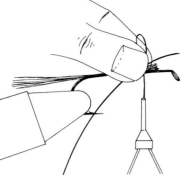

4. Wrap back on both the hackle fibers and the thread.

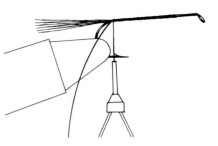

5. Dub a section of the thread on your bobbin (see Pattern 2 for dubbing instructions).

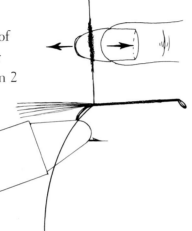

6. Wind forward to two eyewidths behind the eye with the dubbed thread, adding more dubbing if necessary.

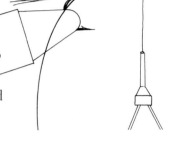

7. Spiral the tying thread forward and tie it down with the bobbin thread.

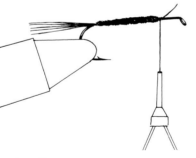

8. Cut a 2" length of polypropylene yarn and tie it down, as shown, to begin the wings.

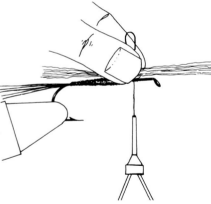

9. Twist the wings so that they are perpendicular to the hook shank, as shown in this overhead view.

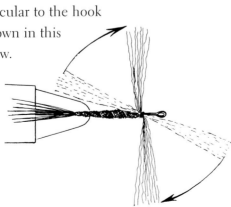

10. Make 3 or 4 wraps diagonally across the hook shank with your bobbin thread so that the thread on the near side is in front of the wing and the thread on the back side is behind the wing.

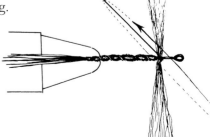

11. Make 3 or 4 wraps diagonally across the hook shank so that the thread on the near side of the hook shank is behind the wing and the thread on the back side is in front of the wing.

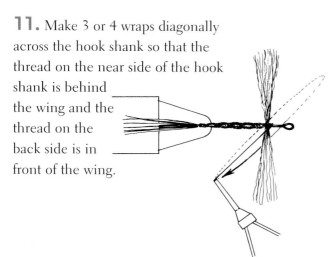

12. Pull the two wing sections upright.

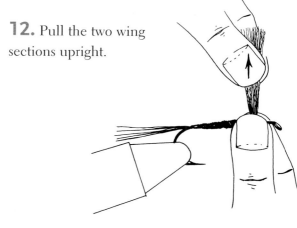

13. Cut the wing height to a length equal to the distance from the back of the eye to the start of the bend (or double the gap of the hook).

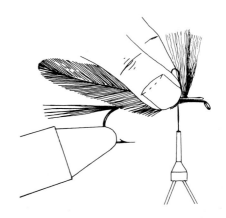

14. Tie in a dry-fly hackle behind the wing with a couple of soft loops and 3 or 4 wraps of thread.

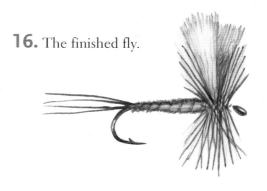

15. Wrap the thread forward, until it is one eye-width behind the eye. Wind the hackle forward, tie it down, and trim off the hackle tip. Form a neat head and whip finish it (see Pattern 15 for whip-finishing instructions).

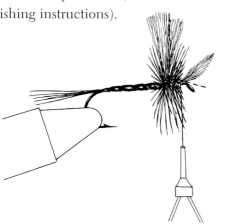

16. The finished fly.

PATTERN

29

WOOLLY BUGGER

HERE'S AN EASY TIE THAT YOU WILL FIND VERY PRODUCTIVE, called a Woolly Bugger. We don't know what it represents, but we suspect that it is one of those patterns that, although not imitative of anything, are suggestive of a lot of food forms that the trout sees, such as large nymphs, minnows, and leeches. We've had good luck fishing it as a streamer, dead drifting it as a nymph, and imparting just a little rising action to it like an emerging insect. Some of the largest trout we have taken couldn't resist our Woolly Buggers. Black hackle on a black or olive body; brown hackle on a brown body; and grizzly hackle on a black, brown, or olive body—all are good producers at times.

1. Attach tying thread two eyewidths back of the eye.

2. Wet a marabou plume and trim off the tip and butt as shown. Tie down the butt end at the tie-in point.

3. Tie in 6 to 8 Flashabou or Crystalhair strands.

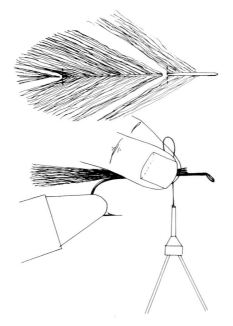

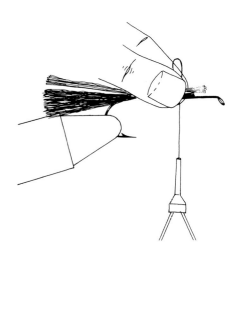

4. Wrap back on the material to a point directly opposite the point of the barb.

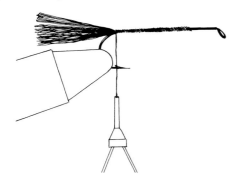

5. Tie in a 6" long piece of chenille.

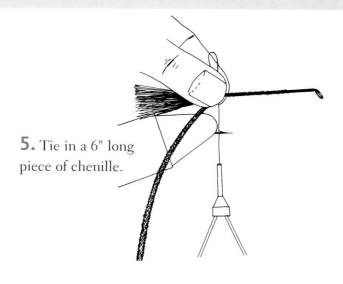

6. Tie in a large, soft hackle feather at the same place.

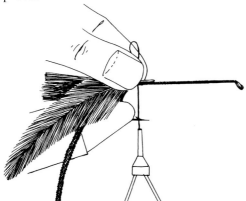

7. Wrap the thread forward to one eyewidth behind the eye.

8. Wind the chenille forward, tie it down, and trim off the excess chenille.

9. Palmer the hackle forward, tie it down, and trim off the hackle tip.

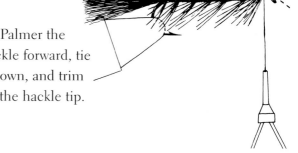

10. Form a neat head and whip finish it (see Pattern 15 for whip-finishing details).

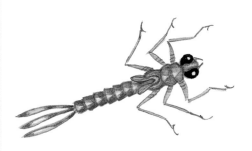

DAMSELFLY NYMPH

WE'RE GOING TO HAVE YOU GET A LITTLE FANCY with this pattern, a damselfly nymph. We'll be using several techniques that you have already learned, but we'll have you put some eyes on this fly and add some weight to the hook. You'll note that we're only adding the weight to the front of the hook. That's because the natural insect typically comes to the surface in a series of rises and descents. If it is front-weighted, our imitation will quickly dive nose-first when we stop our retrieve and then rise when we retrieve it again. Take your time with this one, it's a beautiful fly when tied neatly.

1. Attach the thread halfway between the back of the eye and the point of the hook.

2. Tie in a bunch of marabou, remembering to use a soft loop (see Pattern 2 for details).

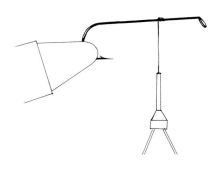

3. Wrap the thread back to opposite the point of the barb and then wrap the thread forward.

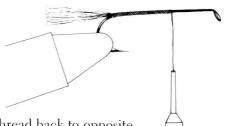

4. Wrap a thin lead wire from the tie-in point to one eyewidth back of the eye. Wrap the thread forward over the lead wire.

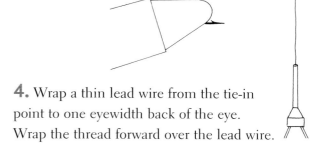

5. Cut two beads from a piece of bead chain, and attach them on the top of the hook by figure-eighting the thread across the piece of wire holding the beads together. Wrap the thread back to the original tie-in point.

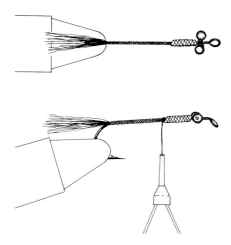

6. Cover the lead wire and tying thread with head cement.

7. Tie in a 6" length of fine copper or brass wire.

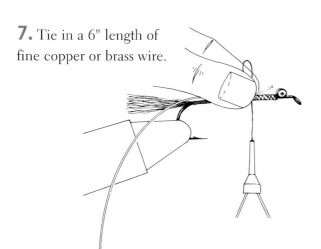

8. Wrap back over the wire with thread to directly opposite the point of the barb. Begin dubbing the tying thread (see Pattern 2 for dubbing details).

9. Wrap the dubbed thread forward to the original tie-in point. Remember, you'll probably need to dub several times to wrap the full length of the body.

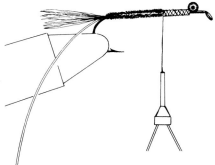

10. Spiral the wire forward, tie it down, and trim off the excess wire.

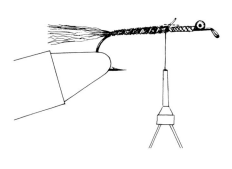

11. Tie in a narrow section of Swiss Straw above the body, using a soft loop. The Swiss Straw should extend from before the eye to the end of the marabou.

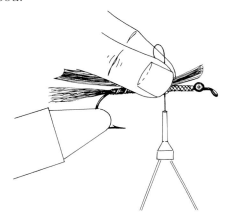

12. Wrap the thread forward over the Swiss Straw to just behind the eye of the hook and then wrap it back to just over the start of the dubbed body. Trim off any excess Swiss Straw.

13. Dub the tying thread rather heavily.

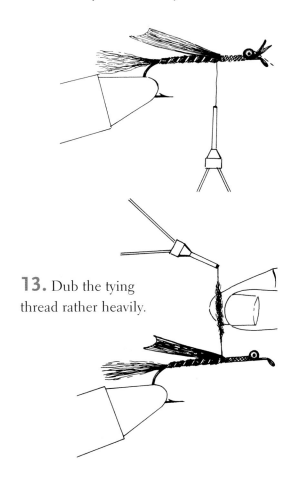

14. Wind it forward to just behind the bead eyes.

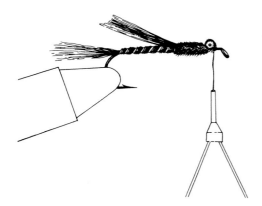

15. Fold the Swiss Straw forward, tie it down behind the eyes, and trim off the excess.

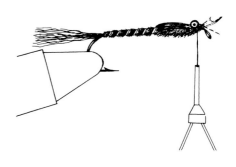

16. Invert the hook in the vise. Tie in 8 to 10 soft hackle fibers on the underside of the hook.

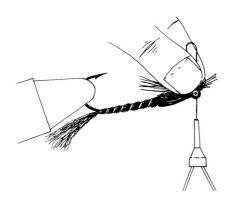

17. Turn the hook upright in the vise. Form a neat head and whip finish to complete the fly.

PATTERN
31

BEAD-HEAD
NYMPH

ADDING A BEAD TO THE HEAD OF A FLY, as we are doing in this pattern, serves a couple of possible purposes. First, it provides a different profile to our fly and imitates the large head seen on many nymphs. Second, it adds weight to the fly; we can choose how much weight by selecting different types of beads: plastic, copper, or tungsten. Plastic beads add very little weight, whereas tungsten is very heavy.

We can also choose the look we want, as plastic beads are available in many colors and metal beads are available in metallic finishes of nickel, copper, brass, gold, and black. The hole through the bead has been drilled from each side, with the hole on one side larger than the other. That's necessary to allow the bead to go around the bend of the hook.

You can add a bead to virtually any nymph pattern to change its appearance and behavior in the water as a result of the weight.

1. Mount the hook in the vise with the point up as shown.

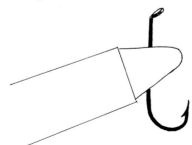

2. Crimp down the barb with your pliers.

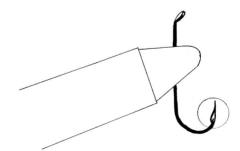

3. Pick up a bead with your pliers (or fingers) and drop the bead over the hook point with its large hole up.

4. Remount the hook in its normal position.

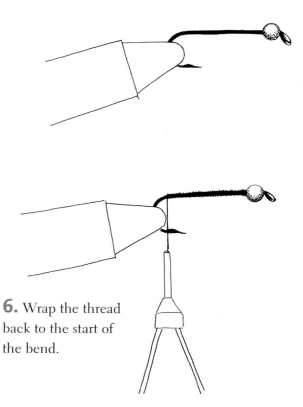

5. Attach the tying thread behind the bead and wrap thread as necessary to hold the bead in position.

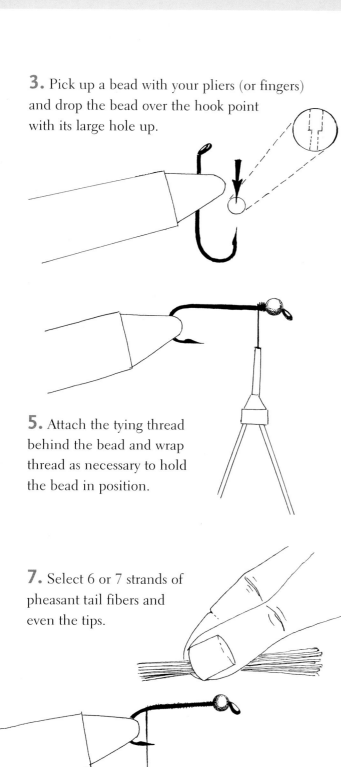

6. Wrap the thread back to the start of the bend.

7. Select 6 or 7 strands of pheasant tail fibers and even the tips.

8. Tie in the pheasant fibers to form a tail with a length equal to one-fourth of the hook shank.

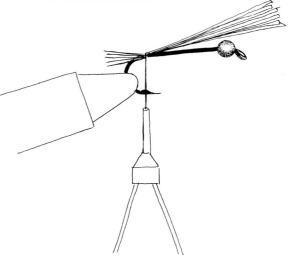

9. Tie in a 6" piece of wire.

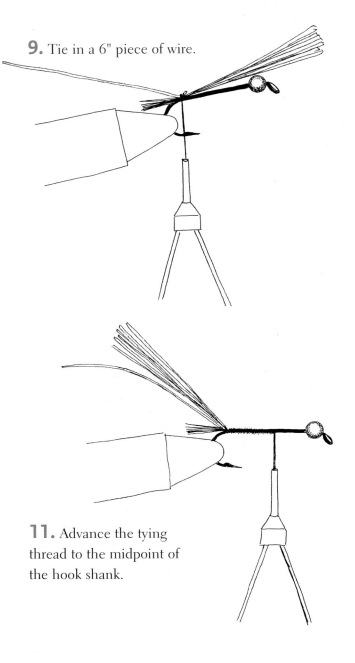

10. Fold the pheasant fibers back and wrap with two turns of thread.

11. Advance the tying thread to the midpoint of the hook shank.

12. Wrap the pheasant forward and tie down where you stopped the thread.

13. Wrap the wire forward in the opposite rotation, tie down, and trim off the excess.

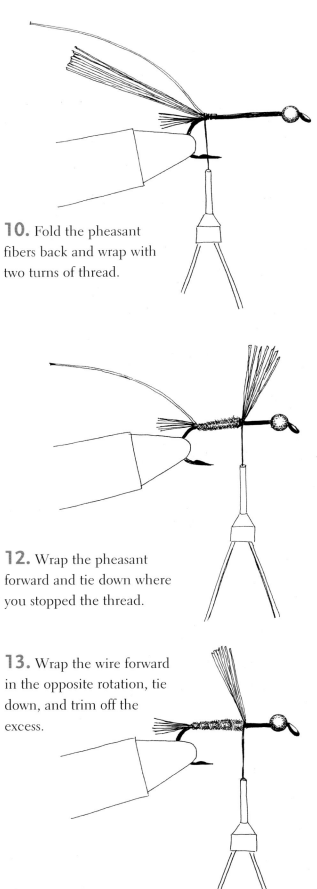

14. Fold the pheasant back and wrap with a couple of turns of thread.

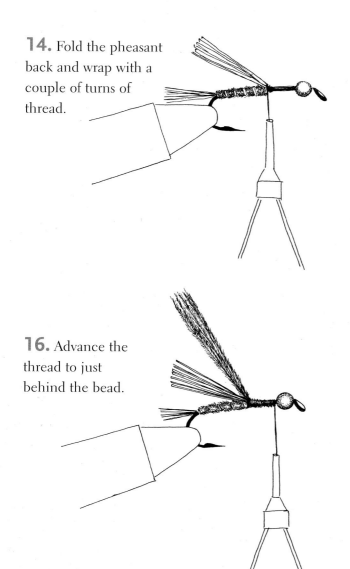

15. Select 5 or 6 strands of peacock herl and tie in.

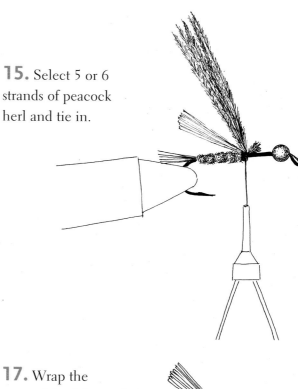

16. Advance the thread to just behind the bead.

17. Wrap the peacock herl forward and tie down.

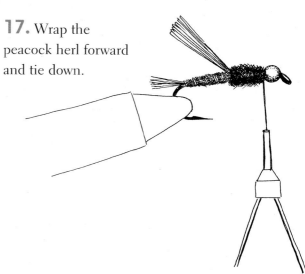

18. Pull the pheasant fibers forward over the peacock to form a wing case, tie down, and trim off the excess. Whip finish.

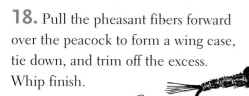

19. The finished fly.

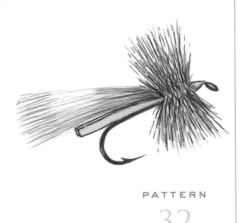

FOAM-BODIED
DRY FLY

HERE IS A GREAT PATTERN THAT ALLOWS YOU TO MATCH any stonefly or caddisfly adult by simply changing the color of the hackle and the foam used for the body. Just trim the foam a little shorter and match its length with the hair wing, and you'll have a great caddis imitation. Use a longer-shanked hook and it will match any stonefly. We tie it with a yellow body for our local yellow stoneflies and with a black body for the great caddis hatch on Colorado's Arkansas River. The fly is very durable and floats extremely well.

You can trim the thin strip of foam from the sheet with your scissors, but a quicker, neater method is to use a razor blade and a straightedge. Be sure to get a smooth taper from where the wing is tied in to the back of the eye … it makes wrapping the hackle much easier.

1. Attach the thread at the midpoint of the hook shank.

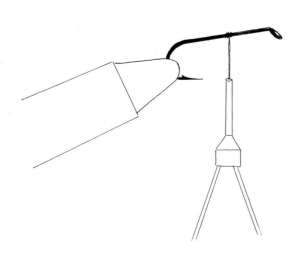

2. Cut a thin strip from the sheet of 2 mm closed-cell foam and attach a short piece of the foam at the tie-in point. The foam should extend just beyond the rear of the hook.

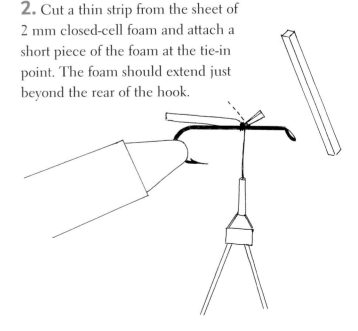

3. Wrap thread to cover the hook shank forward of the foam tie-in point. Cut a small section of elk hair and even the ends in your hair stacker.

4. Tie in the elk hair just forward of the foam tie-in point using a soft loop.

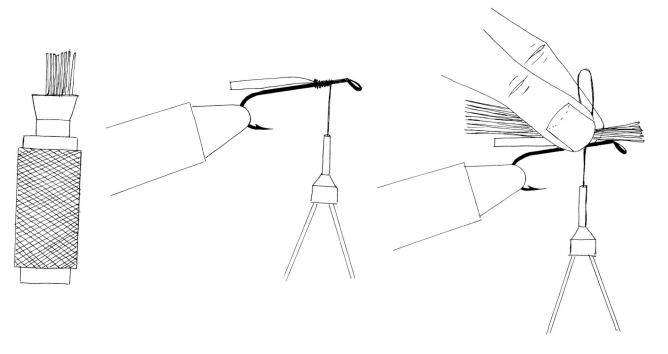

5. Lift the butts of the elk hair and trim as shown (dashed line).

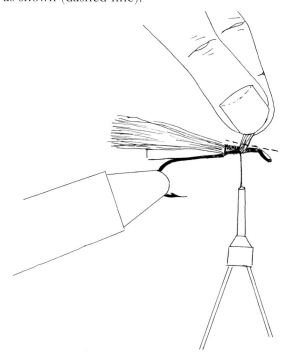

6. Hold the wing firmly in place and make several tight wraps to anchor the wing. Wrap the thread to form a tapered section on the hook as shown.

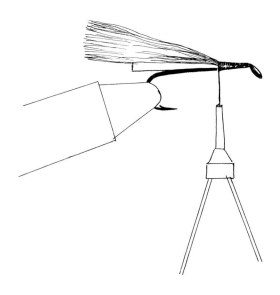

7. Tie in one hackle with the shiny side towards you (hackle #1) and another with the dull side towards you (hackle #2).

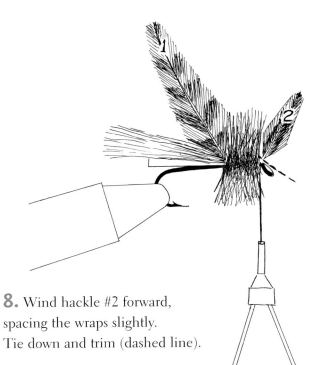

8. Wind hackle #2 forward, spacing the wraps slightly. Tie down and trim (dashed line).

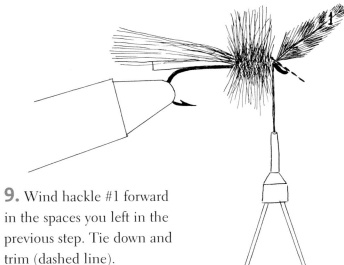

9. Wind hackle #1 forward in the spaces you left in the previous step. Tie down and trim (dashed line).

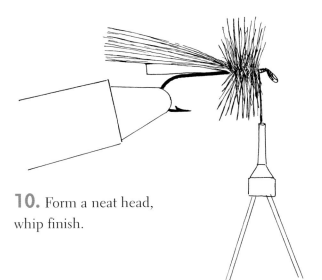

10. Form a neat head, whip finish.

11. The finished fly.

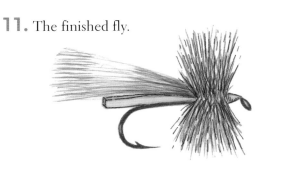

CHART OF PATTERNS

1 *Simple caddisfly larva*

2 *Midge larva*

3 *Simple mayfly nymph*

4 *Stonefly nymph*

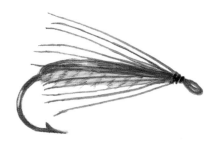

5 *Caddisfly pupa*

6 *Midge pupa*

7 *Mayfly emerger*

8 *Mayfly adult with quill wing*

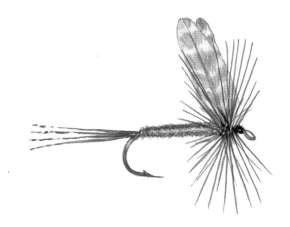

9 *Mayfly adult with hackle-tip wing*

10 *Mayfly adult with rolled wing*

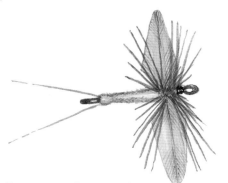

11 *Mayfly imago (spinner) stage*

12 *Stonefly adult*

13 *Caddisfly adult*

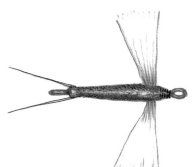

14 *Midge adult*

15 *Hair-wing streamer*

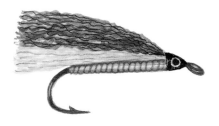

16 *Marabou streamer*

17 *Hackle-wing streamer*

18 *Spun-hair streamer (muddler minnow)*

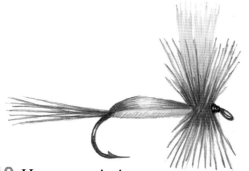

19 *Humpy variation*

20 *Shrimp or scud (gammarus)*

21 *Simple wet-fly attractor*

22 *Dry-fly attractor*

23 *Wet-fly attractor (Rio Grande king)*

24 *Wet-fly attractor (salmon-fly type)*

25 *Matuka*

26 *Zonker*

27 *Golden stonefly nymph*

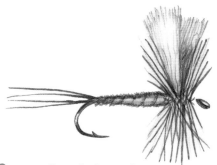

28 *Mayfly adult with polypropylene wing*

29 Woolly bugger

30 Damselfly nymph

31 *Bead-head nymph*

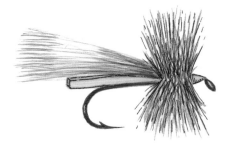

32 *Foam-bodied dry fly*

GLOSSARY

abdomen: The rear body portion of an insect.

adult: The last stage in the life of an insect; for aquatic insects, the stage spent out of the water.

alderfly: A member of the insect order Megaloptera, family Sialidae. They undergo complete metamorphosis.

Anisoptera: The suborder of the insect order Odonata that includes dragonflies.

attractor: A fly that does not represent a specific food form.

badger: Body hair or dubbing from a badger; a cream to ginger hackle with a black center stripe.

baitfish: Any of the small fish or minnows that are available as food to fish.

barb: The rear tip of a hook point; the individual fibers extending from the shaft of a feather.

beetle: The common name for members of the insect order Coleoptera. There are both aquatic and terrestrial beetles that may be of importance to the fly-tyer.

bend: The curve at the rear of the hook that establishes the gap; the shape of the bend; i.e., perfect bend, sproat bend, etc.

bead head: A fly tied with a metal or plastic bead behind the hook eye.

bobbin: A tool for holding a spool of tying thread under tension.

bodkin: A needle-like tool often used in fly-tying.

bucktail: The hair taken from the tail of a white-tailed deer; a type of streamer fly that uses bucktail for the wing.

caddisfly: Various flies of the order Trichoptera. Caddisflies undergo complete metamorphosis. The adult carries its wings over its back in an inverted V.

calf tail: The hair from a calf's tail, also called kip or impala.

cape: Another term for a hackle neck.

coachman: A hackle of very dark brown.

coch-y-bonddu: A hackle in the shades from dark ginger to brown with a black center stripe and black edges.

Coleoptera: The order of insects that includes all beetles. They undergo complete metamorphosis. Some are aquatic.

complete metamorphosis: The life cycle of insects that pass through four distinct stages: egg, larva, pupa, and adult.

crane fly: An insect of the order Diptera, family Tipulidae, that resembles a large mosquito in the adult stage. It undergoes complete metamorphosis.

cream: Color of hackle ranging from just darker than white to a pale yellow.

Crystalhair: A translucent, synthetic hair.

damselfly: A large aquatic insect of the order Odonata, suborder Zygoptera, that resembles its relative the dragonfly. It undergoes incomplete metamorphosis.

Diptera: An order of insects having two wings. They undergo complete metamorphosis. Diptera are generally small to moderate in size. Crane flies (Tipulidae, "daddy long-legs") are a notable exception. Mosquitoes, house flies, black flies, and midges are Dipterans.

dobson fly: Large insects of the order Megaloptera, genus Corydalis. The nymphs are often called hellgrammites.

down-eye hook: A hook with the eye bent below the shank; abbreviated TDE (turned-down eye).

dragonfly: A large aquatic insect of the order Odonata, suborder Anisoptera, which closely resembles its close relative the damselfly. The dragonfly undergoes incomplete metamorphosis.

drake: A common term for the adult male mayfly.

dry fly: A fly tied to represent the adult stage of an insect.

dubbing: (1) The process of spinning fur onto the tying thread to form a "yarn" of fur for making the body of a fly; (2) any material used for dubbing.

dun: (1) A hackle of neutral gray/brown; it may have overtones of blue, olive, or bronze; (2) the first adult stage (subimago stage) of a mayfly.

emerger: A term used loosely to describe any insect that moves up towards the water's surface preparatory to hatching into the adult stage.

Ephemeroptera: An order of insects comprising the mayflies. They undergo incomplete metamorphosis. The adult has an upright wing.

eye: (1) The loop at the end of the hook shank to which the leader is attached; (2) the feathers or painted dots at the head of some streamer patterns that are meant to imitate a minnow's eyes.

fine: A relative measurement of hook wire diameter. For example, a #14 2X fine hook is a number 14 hook made from wire normally used for a hook two sizes smaller (#16).

Flashabou: A ribbon-shaped, tinsel-like synthetic material used in attractor-type streamers.

floss: A heavy silk or rayon thread used primarily as a body material.

freshwater shrimp: Small aquatic crustaceans that are a prime food source for trout in some areas.

furnace: A hackle ranging in color from dark ginger to brown, with a black center stripe.

gap: The distance from the shank to the point of the hook.

ginger: A color of hackle ranging from light to medium brown with a tinge of red.

grannom: A common term for a caddisfly.

grizzly: A black or dark gray hackle with white bars; it is sometimes called Plymouth Rock after the breed of chicken that produces it.

guard hair: The coarse, long hair on an animal's pelt.

hackle: (1) A feather from the neck or rump of a chicken; (2) a feather wound on a hook edgewise; (3) the act of putting a hackle on a fly.

hackle gauge: A small, ruler-like tool marked to measure the correct size of hackle for a given size of fly.

hackle guard: A small, funnel-shaped tool for holding the hackle away from the head area while the head of the fly is being formed and tied off.

hackle pliers: A tool used to grasp a hackle for winding.

hackle-tip wing: A type of wing construction using two hackle tips to form the wings.

hair stacker: A tool used to align the ends of a bunch of hair.

hair-wing: A dry-fly type that uses a divided, evened bunch of hair to form the wings.

half hitch: An easy, although inferior method of tying off thread, for example at the head of a fly.

half-hitch tool: A tool designed to aid the forming of half hitches.

hen: A female insect. The term is normally used in reference to mayflies.

herl: A long, thin feather, such as peacock, ostrich, or emu, which creates a "fuzzy" appearance when wrapped on a hook.

imago: (1) An insect in its final adult, sexually mature, usually winged, stage; (2) the second, and final adult stage of the mayfly, at which time it is also called a spinner.

impala: Another name for calf hair.

incomplete metamorphosis: The life cycle of insects that pass through only three stages—egg, nymph, and the adult.

jungle cock: The feather from the breast of a gray jungle fowl (*Gallus sonnerati*) that was commonly used for the eye on salmon and streamer flies; it is now rare.

kip: Another name for calf tail.

larva: The second stage in complete metamorphosis. The insect is a larva after being an egg and before being a pupa. Larvae generally are wormlike in appearance.

list: The stripe of contrasting color on the edge of a feather.

long: A relative measurement of hook length. For example, a #14 2X long hook is a #14 hook that is as long as a hook two sizes longer (a #12).

marabou: A very soft, long-fibered feather from a white turkey. Dyed to desired colors, it is used primarily for streamers as it has a "breathing" action in the water.

mask: The face skin of an animal, most commonly a rabbit or hare.

material clip: A device that attaches just behind the vise jaws to hold tied-in material out of the way while the tyer performs other steps in the tying process.

mayfly: The common name for insects of the order Ephemeroptera. They undergo incomplete metamorphosis. The adult has an upright wing.

metamorphosis: The form changes occurring in the life cycle of an insect—for example, from larva to pupa to adult, or from nymph to adult.

midge: "Midge" is the common term for insects of the order Diptera, families Chironomidae (true midges) and Ceratopogonidae (biting midges). Midges undergo complete metamorphosis and generally are very small. Gnats, smuts, and snow flies are midges.

Mylar: A flexible plastic material with a metallized finish, available in many forms including sheets, braided tubing, and tinsel.

neck: The neck skin of a bird, usually a chicken, with the feathers (hackle) attached; also called a cape.

no-hackle fly: A type of dry fly, popularized by Swisher and Richards, which doesn't use hackle as the support for the floating fly.

nymph: (1) A stage in the incomplete metamorphosis of an insect that comes after the egg and before the adult. (2) An artificial fly fished as an imitation of a nymph, larva, or pupa.

Odonata: An order of insects including the dragonflies and damselflies; they undergo incomplete metamorphosis.

oviposit: The act of laying eggs, particularly among insects.

palmered: A fly with a hackle wound in a spiral for the full length of the hook shank.

periwinkle: A colloquial term for an encased caddisfly larva or pupa.

Plecoptera: An order of insects commonly called stoneflies. They undergo incomplete metamorphosis. The adult carries its wings flat over its back.

Plymouth Rock: (1) The chicken that produces grizzly hackle; (2) another name for grizzly hackle.

point: The sharp tip of a hook.

pointer: The feathers at the very tip of a bird's wing, e.g., duck pointer or goose pointer. Pointers are used as the source of quill segments for tying quill wings.

polypropylene: A synthetic material used as dubbing or for wings, available in pressed sheets, as yarn, or as loose dubbing. It is a very effective body material for dry flies as it has a specific gravity of less than one.

poly-wing: A dry fly tied with polypropylene yarn for the wings.

pupa: The stage in the complete metamorphosis of an insect that comes between the larval and adult stages.

quill: A feather from the wing of a duck or goose.

quill body: A type of body construction in which stripped peacock herl, stripped hackle, or two or three quill fibers are wrapped around the hook shank to achieve a segmented effect.

quill wing: A wing made from paired quill segments.

ribbing: A thin strip of material wound over the body of a fly in a spiral to produce a segmented effect.

rock worm: A colloquial term for a caddisfly larva or pupa, or the larval stage of the crane fly (order Diptera, family Tipulidae).

rolled wing: A type of wing construction in which a bunch of hackle fibers are divided to form wings.

saddle hackle: The long, slim feathers from the rump of a chicken.

sculpin: A bottom-feeding fish characterized by very large gills; small sculpins are an important food form in many trout streams.

shank: The straight section of a hook from the eye to the bend.

short: A relative measurement of hook length. For example, a #14 short hook is a #14 hook that is of length equal to a hook two sizes shorter (a #16).

spent: Lying with wings outstretched.

spent-wing: A fly tied with the wings in the spent position.

stonefly: An insect of the order Plecoptera. Stoneflies undergo incomplete metamorphosis. The adult carries its wings flat over its back.

stout: A relative measurement of hook wire diameters. For example, a #14 2X stout hook is a #14 hook made from wire normally used for a hook two sizes larger (a #12).

streamer: A type of fly that is tied to be representative of a baitfish.

tail: (1) The tail of a fly; (2) the act of attaching the tail material to the hook.

terrestrial: An insect whose life cycle is completed outside the aquatic environment.

thorax: The area between the head and the abdomen of an insect; the wings are attached to this section.

throat hackle: A small bunch of hackle fibers tied under the hook and extending from just behind the eye to near the point of the hook.

tinsel: A thin metal or metallic plastic strip, usually of gold or silver color, used for fly bodies or ribbing.

Trichoptera: An order of "hairy-winged" insects, including caddisflies. They undergo complete metamorphosis. The adult carries its wings over its back in an inverted "V".

variant: Any hackle with more than one color present, most commonly barred.

vise: The tool used to hold the hook during the tying process.

wet fly: An artificial fly that is fished beneath the water's surface; it is probably taken by the fish to be a nymph or emerging nymph.

whip finish: The preferred method for finishing the head of a fly.

whip-finish tool: A tool designed to aid in tying the whip finish.

wing case: An enlarged area on the top of the insect's thorax that houses the immature wings prior to the adult stage.

Zygoptera: The suborder (of the order Odonata) of insects that includes the damselflies.

METRIC EQUIVALENTS TABLE

INCHES TO MILLIMETERS (MM) AND CENTIMETERS (CM)

Inches	mm	cm	Inches	cm
1/8	3	0.3	9	22.9
1/4	6	0.6	10	25.4
3/8	10	1.0	11	27.9
1/2	13	1.3	12	30.5
5/8	16	1.6	13	33.0
3/4	19	1.9	14	35.6
7/8	22	2.2	15	38.1
1	25	2.5	16	40.6
1 1/4	32	3.2	17	43.2
1 1/2	38	3.8	18	5.7
1 3/4	44	4.4	19	48.3
2	51	5.1	20	50.8
2 1/2	64	6.4	21	53.3
3	76	7.6	22	55.9
3 1/2	89	8.9	23	58.4
4	102	10.2	24	61.0
4 1/2	114	11.4	25	63.5
5	127	12.7	26	66.0
6	152	15.2	27	68.6
7	178	17.8	28	71.1
8	203	20.3	29	73.7

INDEX